# Gourmet ITALIAN

# Gourmet ITALIAN

## All-Time Favorite Recipes

Houghton Mifflin Harcourt
Boston / New York / 2012

Copyright © 2012 by Condé Nast Publications
Photographs copyright © 2012 by Condé Nast Publications
unless otherwise stated
All rights reserved

*Gourmet*® is a registered trademark of Advance Magazine
Publisher, used under license.

The contents of this book previously appeared in various
issues of *Gourmet* magazine and were published in their
entirety in a special edition of *Gourmet* in Winter/Spring 2011
under the same title as this book.

For information about permission to reproduce selections
from this book, write to Permissions, Houghton Mifflin
Harcourt Publishing Company, 215 Park Avenue South,
New York, New York 10003.

www.hmhbooks.com

Library of Congress Cataloging-in-Publication Data
is available.

ISBN 978-0-547-84368-1

Book design by Margaret Swart

For credits, see page 186.

Printed in the United States of America
DOC 10 9 8 7 6 5 4 3 2 1

# CONTENTS

# CONTENTS

# INTRODUCTION

*by Sara Moulton*

## As a kid growing up in New York City, I loved

Italian food even before I knew it was Italian. Pizza, spaghetti and meatballs, and hero sandwiches arrived in the city so long ago that they were like the air we breathed.

And—big surprise—many of my family's favorite local restaurants were Italian. For everyday, we had our choice of several lovely spots on Irving Place, right in the neighborhood. If it was a special occasion, we'd go to Paone's on East 34th Street. Presided over by Nicola Paone himself—a debonair Italian who opened his own restaurant after a successful international career as a singer and actor—Paone's was proof of the appeal of Italian cuisine and its astonishing depth of flavor. Mushrooms, tomatoes, garlic and fresh herbs, olives, capers, sparkling seafood, locally produced meats and cheeses: It's hard to go wrong when ingredients like these are found in such magnificent abundance. The Italians prize these basics, insist on their freshness and seasonality, and have cooked them with love and flair for millennia.

As the chef of *Gourmet*'s executive dining room, charged with delighting the magazine's guests, I turned again and again to *Gourmet*'s Italian recipes, confident that nothing surpassed them when it came to creating the requisite feeling of expansive well-being.

And now, thanks to this book, you can perform exactly the same kind of magic at home. *Gourmet Italian* includes the best of the thousands of Italian and Italian-American recipes to grace the magazine's pages over the decades. You will find quintessential recipes for classics with a twist, such as lasagne Bolognese with spinach, sweet potato gnocchi with fried sage and chestnuts, truffled Taleggio and mushroom pizza, pork chop saltimbocca, and Sunday ragù. There are easy antipasti, little appetizer bites perfect for entertaining, slow-cooked mains, quick stovetop dishes, and a cornucopia of vegetable sides. Topping it all off are a pair of my personal favorites: a perfect tiramisu and a caramel espresso float.

Whether you want to throw together a simple weeknight dinner or prepare a memorable feast for special guests, you will find exactly what you want in *Gourmet Italian*. This book also includes a primer on Italian pantry items and Italian cheeses, as well as instructions for making fresh pasta and can't-live-without pasta sauces to get you through the week. It also boasts a recipe for my favorite secret ingredient: toasted bread crumbs, which add an addictive crunch to any dish.

So what are you waiting for? Between the covers of this book are the keys to *la dolce vita*.

# RECIPE TIPS

▶ **MEASURE LIQUIDS** in a glass or clear plastic liquid-measuring cups and **DRY INGREDIENTS** in nesting dry-measuring cups that can be leveled off with a knife.

▶ **MEASURE FLOUR** by spooning (not scooping) it into a dry-measuring cup and leveling off with a knife; do not tap or shake the cup.

▶ **DO NOT SIFT FLOUR UNLESS** specified in recipe. If sifted flour is called for, sift before measuring. (Disregard "presifted" on the label.)

▶ **SALT:** Measurements are for table salt unless otherwise specified. We don't recommend substituting another type, since the amounts differ when measured by volume.

▶ **BLACK PEPPER** is always freshly ground.

▶ **SPICES:** Store away from heat and light; buy in small quantities.

▶ **TOAST WHOLE SPICES** in a dry heavy skillet over medium heat, stirring, until fragrant and a shade darker, usually 3 to 5 minutes.

▶ **TOAST NUTS** in a shallow baking pan in a 350°F oven until golden, 5 to 15 minutes.

▶ **TOAST SEEDS** like spices or nuts.

▶ **MELT CHOCOLATE** in a metal bowl set over barely simmering water, stirring; or microwave at low to medium power for short intervals (30 seconds or less; stir to check consistency).

▶ **BAKING PANS:** We prefer light-colored metal. If you are using dark metal, including nonstick, your baked goods may brown more, and the cooking times may be shorter. Lower the oven temperature 25°F to compensate.

▶ **NONREACTIVE COOKWARE** includes stainless steel, glass, and enameled cast iron; avoid pure aluminum and uncoated iron, which can impart an unpleasant taste and color to recipes with acidic ingredients.

▶ **WATER BATH FOR BAKING:** Put the filled pan in a larger pan and place in oven, then add enough boiling water to reach halfway up the side of the smaller pan.

▶ **PRODUCE:** Thoroughly wash and dry all produce before using.

▶ **GREENS AND CHOPPED/SLICED LEEKS:** Submerge in a large bowl of water, agitating them, then lift out and drain well. If the water in the bowl is dirty, repeat. Pat leeks dry on towels. For greens, spin dry in a spinner several times, stopping to pour off collected water.

▶ **FRESH HERBS OR GREENS:** Use only the leaves and tender stems.

▶ **CITRUS ZEST:** Remove the colored part of the rind only (avoid the bitter white pith). For strips, use a vegetable peeler. For grating, we prefer a rasplike Microplane zester, which results in fluffier zest, so pack to measure.

▶ **CHILES:** Wear protective gloves when handling, and avoid touching your face.

## To Grill

▶ **CHARCOAL GRILLING INSTRUCTIONS:** Open the vents on the bottom of the grill. Light a large chimney starter full of charcoal.

▶ **FOR DIRECT-HEAT COOKING:** When the coals are lit, dump them out across the bottom rack, leaving a space free of coals equal to the size of the food to be grilled where you can move the food in case of any flare-ups.

▶ **FOR INDIRECT-HEAT COOKING:** When the coals are lit, dump them out along two opposite sides of bottom rack, leaving a space free of charcoal in the middle of the rack equal to the size of the food to be grilled.

▶ **FOR DIRECT- OR INDIRECT-HEAT COOKING:** When the charcoal turns grayish white, the grill will be at its hottest. How long you can hold your hand 5 inches above the grill rack directly over the coals determines the heat of your grill, as follows:

HOT: 1 to 2 seconds
MEDIUM HOT: 3 to 4 seconds
LOW: 5 to 6 seconds

▶ **GAS GRILL INSTRUCTIONS** Preheat all burners on high, covered, for 10 minutes, then adjust the heat according to the recipe. For indirect-heat cooking, just before grilling, turn off one burner (the middle burner if there are three).

< *Fava-Bean
Crostini,
page 18*

# CHAPTER 1

# ANTIPASTI

Just as every journey begins with a step, every meal is launched with a single bite. In Italy, that first morsel is likely to be intensely flavorful—a slice of salami, a handful of olives, crostini rubbed with fragrant garlic—to stimulate the palate for the adventure to come. Traditionally, antipasti are served on platters and eaten by everyone gathered around the table, symbolizing the companionship at the heart of a meal ("companion" comes from the Latin word meaning "to share bread"). But these rustic, room-temperature dishes are so easy to make and serve that we've adapted them to our relaxed, stand-around-the-kitchen style of entertaining. Wherever a feast takes you, these antipasti will feel right at home.

# Orange Negronis

*Adapted from Tony Oltranti*

Serves **2** | Active time: **5 minutes** | Start to finish: **5 minutes**

We added freshly squeezed orange juice to a traditional Italian aperitif and served it straight up in a chilled martini glass. *Salute!*

3  **ounces (6 tablespoons) gin**
3  **ounces (6 tablespoons) Campari**
3  **ounces (6 tablespoons) sweet (red) vermouth**
2  **splashes fresh orange juice**
**SPECIAL EQUIPMENT**
   **Cocktail shaker**
**GARNISH**
   **Orange twists**

▶ Combine all ingredients with ice in shaker. Shake well and strain into chilled martini glasses. Garnish each glass with an orange twist.

**COOKS' NOTE:** The orange twists give the Negronis fragrance and flavor.

# Roasted Hazelnuts with Thyme

*Adapted from Holly Smith*

**Makes 2 cups** | **Active time: 15 minutes** | **Start to finish: 45 minutes**

- 2 cups hazelnuts (10 ounces)
- 2 tablespoons fresh thyme leaves
- 2 tablespoons extra-virgin olive oil
  Coarse sea salt such as Maldon or *fleur de sel* to taste

▶ Preheat oven to 450°F, with rack in middle.

▶ Roast nuts in a single layer in a shallow baking pan in oven until nuts have a toasted aroma and skins are very dark, about 8 minutes. Remove from oven and let stand 30 minutes, then, if desired, rub in a kitchen towel to remove any loose skins.

▶ Heat nuts with thyme in oil in a large heavy skillet over medium heat, shaking skillet, just until hot. Transfer to a bowl and sprinkle with sea salt.

**COOKS' NOTE:** The nuts can be roasted 1 day ahead and kept covered.

You'll reach for this recipe again and again for its stunning simplicity and the way it pairs perfectly with any aperitif. Roasting the hazelnuts in the oven results in a deep nuttiness, which is then brought firmly into the savory realm with a sprinkling of salt and thyme.

# Garlic Knots

Makes **5 dozen** | Active time: **40 minutes** | Start to finish: **1 hour**

Be sure to make enough for a crowd, because these chewy, garlicky knots—a pizzeria classic—will go fast.

2 tablespoons olive oil, plus additional for greasing pan
2 pounds pizza dough, thawed completely if frozen
1 garlic clove
¼ teaspoon salt
1 tablespoon finely chopped fresh flat-leaf parsley
½ cup grated Parmigiano-Reggiano

▶ Preheat oven to 400°F, with racks in upper and lower thirds. Lightly oil two large baking sheets.

▶ Divide dough in half. Keep half of dough covered with a clean kitchen towel (not terry cloth). Gently roll out other half into a 10-inch square on a lightly floured surface with a lightly floured rolling pin. (Use your hands to pull corners. If dough is very elastic, cover with a clean kitchen towel and let rest for about 3 minutes.)

▶ Cut square in half with a pizza wheel or a sharp heavy knife, then cut each half crosswise into 15 strips (about ⅔-inch wide). Cover strips with a clean kitchen towel.

▶ Keeping remaining strips covered, gently tie each strip into a knot, pulling ends slightly to secure (if dough is sticky, dust lightly with flour) and arranging knots 1 inch apart in staggered rows on 1 baking sheet. Keep knots covered with clean kitchen towels. Repeat with remaining dough on second baking sheet.

▶ Bake, switching position of sheets halfway through baking, until golden, 20 to 25 minutes total.

▶ While knots bake, mince garlic and mash to a paste with salt, then stir together with oil in a very large bowl. Immediately after baking, toss knots in garlic oil, then sprinkle with parsley and cheese and toss to coat. Serve warm or at room temperature.

**COOKS' NOTE:** The knots can be baked, but not coated, 2 hours ahead. Reheat the knots on a large baking sheet in a preheated 350°F oven until hot, 3 to 5 minutes, then toss with garlic oil, parsley, and cheese.

# Fava-Bean Crostini

Serves 8 | Active time: **30 minutes** | Start to finish: **30 minutes**

The favorite Tuscan springtime snack of young green fava beans with salty, nutty crumbles of Pecorino Toscano—a firm sheep's milk cheese—is the inspiration for these savory little toasts. Fresh arugula, both pureed and roughly chopped, punctuates the spread with spice and texture. If you can't find fresh favas, fresh or frozen edamame work well, too.

- 1 cup shelled fresh fava beans (1¼ pounds in pods) or shelled fresh or frozen edamame (soybeans; ¾ pound in pods)
- ¼ cup plus 1 tablespoon extra-virgin olive oil
- 1½ cups packed baby arugula, chopped
- 3 tablespoons grated Pecorino Toscano or Parmigiano-Reggiano
- ¼ teaspoon grated lemon zest
- ½ teaspoon fresh lemon juice
- ½ teaspoon salt
- ⅛ teaspoon black pepper
- 1 baguette
- 1 garlic clove, halved crosswise
- 16 fresh mint leaves

▶ Preheat oven to 350°F, with rack in middle.

▶ Cook beans in boiling water, uncovered, until tender, 3 to 4 minutes, then drain and transfer to an ice bath to stop cooking. Gently peel off skins (if using edamame, don't peel).

▶ Pulse beans in a food processor until very coarsely chopped, then transfer half to a bowl. Add ¼ cup oil, ⅓ cup arugula, cheese, lemon zest and juice, salt, and pepper to processor and puree. Add to bowl. Fold in remaining arugula.

▶ Cut 16 diagonal slices (⅓-inch thick) from baguette and put on a baking sheet. Bake until golden, 8 to 10 minutes. Rub with cut side of garlic, and drizzle with some of the remaining oil.

▶ Spoon fava-bean mixture onto baguette toasts, then drizzle with additional oil and top with mint.

# Asparagus and Prosciutto Bruschette

*Adapted from Rose Gray and Ruth Rogers*

Serves **6** | Active time: **20 minutes** | Start to finish: **25 minutes**

Be sure to use high-quality olive oil. We love the green peppery oils from Tuscany (for more on when to break out the good stuff, see page 182). Drizzle the oil on the bread after grilling so you can taste its complexity.

1 **pound thin asparagus, trimmed**
6 **(½-inch-thick) slices sourdough bread, cut from middle of a halved 8- to 9-inch round loaf**
1 **large garlic clove, halved crosswise**
  **Maldon sea salt**
  **Coarsely ground black pepper**
3 **tablespoons extra-virgin olive oil**
1 **teaspoon red-wine vinegar**
2 **cups baby arugula**
2 **ounces thinly sliced prosciutto**

▶ Bring 1½ inches salted water to a boil in a 12-inch skillet, then add asparagus and cook over medium heat until just tender, 3 to 7 minutes. Drain asparagus in a colander and return to skillet off heat.

▶ Meanwhile, heat a lightly oiled large ridged grill pan over medium-high heat until hot and just beginning to smoke. Grill bread slices (in batches if necessary) until pale golden and grill marks appear, about 45 seconds to 1 minute per side. Lightly rub 1 side of each toast with cut side of a garlic half, then season with sea salt and pepper to taste and drizzle with oil (about 1 teaspoon per slice).

▶ Season asparagus with sea salt and pepper, then drizzle with vinegar and remaining tablespoon oil. Add arugula and toss gently to coat, then divide mixture among toasts along with prosciutto.

KITCHEN TIP
## THE RIGHT BREAD

Great bruschette begins with great bread. You want a loaf that has not only a good crust but a sturdy—though light and porous—crumb. Sourdough loaves are your best bet because the long, slow rise allows the dough to develop real structure, which you need if the bread is going to stand up to the garlic treatment. Once you grill or toast the sourdough slices, the surface of the toast will crisp up to an almost sandpaper-like texture, perfect for grabbing and holding the bits of raw garlic as you rub the cut sides of the clove over the bread. Flimsy loaves need not apply.

# Slow-Roasted-Tomato Bruschette

*Adapted from Tony Oltranti*

Makes **16** | Active time: **15 minutes** | Start to finish: **7 to 9 hours**

Toasted or grilled country-style bread drizzled with olive oil and topped with juicy tomatoes is a Tuscan classic.

- **4 pounds plum tomatoes, halved lengthwise**
- **6 garlic cloves, minced**
- **8 tablespoons extra-virgin olive oil**
- **Salt and black pepper**
- **16 (½-inch-thick) slices good-quality Italian bread, preferably cut from a long loaf**

▶ Preheat oven to 200°F, with racks in upper and lower thirds.
▶ Put tomatoes, cut sides up, on two large baking sheets. Combine garlic and 5 tablespoons oil and spoon over tomatoes. Season tomatoes with salt and pepper and roast in oven, switching position of sheets halfway through roasting, 6 to 8 hours (tomatoes will shrink but retain their shape). Cool tomatoes.
▶ Increase oven to 350°F.
▶ Arrange bread in one layer on two large baking sheets and bake, switching position of sheets halfway through, until golden and crisp, 10 to 15 minutes.
▶ Brush toasts with remaining 3 tablespoons oil and top with 2 to 3 roasted tomato halves.

**COOKS' NOTE:** The roasted tomatoes keep in an airtight container, chilled, for 2 weeks. Bring to room temperature before using.

# Prosciutto-Wrapped Grissini

*Adapted from Holly Smith*

Makes **12** | Active time: **10 minutes** | Start to finish: **10 minutes**

This classic appetizer showcases prosciutto's buttery texture and oaky sweetness. Its success will depend on your prosciutto, so look for imported Parma such as prosciutto di Rotondo or San Daniele or an excellent domestic brand such as La Quercia.

12   thin slices prosciutto di Parma
12   *grissini*

▶ Wrap a slice of prosciutto around upper portion of each breadstick at an angle, slightly overlapping.

**COOKS' NOTE:** The *grissini* can be wrapped 30 minutes ahead and kept, loosely covered, at room temperature.

# Mushroom Carpaccio

½ pound large white mushrooms
1½ tablespoons fresh lemon juice
½ pound piece of Pecorino Toscano
    or Parmigiano-Reggiano
3 tablespoons extra-virgin olive oil
¼ cup tender inner celery leaves
    Flaky sea salt, such as Maldon
**SPECIAL EQUIPMENT**
    **Adjustable-blade slicer**

▶ Slice mushrooms lengthwise as thinly as possible with slicer.
▶ Spread mushrooms out on a large platter and drizzle with lemon juice. Using a vegetable peeler, shave some cheese over top. Drizzle with oil and sprinkle with celery leaves. Season with sea salt.

**COOKS' NOTE:** The mushrooms can be sliced 1 hour ahead and chilled, covered with damp paper towels.

The salads of shaved raw porcini mushrooms that are served throughout Italy are the inspiration for this version made with large, firm white mushrooms. A big squeeze of lemon juice and a scattering of herbaceous celery leaves contribute brightness. Speedy yet luxurious, this may become your new party dish.

# Bresaola Carpaccio with Caper and Egg Vinaigrette

**Serves 6 to 8** | Active time: **30 minutes** | Start to finish: **30 minutes**

Top *bresaola*—a beef lover's prosciutto equivalent—with peppery arugula and a briny egg dressing for a virtually no-cook antipasto.

- **2 hard-boiled large eggs, quartered**
- **½ cup minced radishes (about 4)**
- **2 tablespoons drained capers (in brine), rinsed and chopped**
- **2 tablespoons minced cornichons or pickles (not sweet)**
- **2 tablespoons chopped fresh chives**
- **1½ tablespoons fresh lemon juice**
- **½ teaspoon salt, or to taste**
- **¼ teaspoon black pepper, or to taste**
- **3 tablespoons extra-virgin olive oil**
- **10 ounces thinly sliced air-dried beef, such as *bresaola* or *Bundnerfleisch*, or prosciutto**
- **5 ounces baby arugula (7½ cups)**
- **2 tablespoons grated Parmigiano-Reggiano**

▸ Force eggs through a medium-mesh sieve into a small bowl using back of a spoon.

▸ Add radishes, capers, cornichons, and chives to eggs, then gently toss to combine.

▸ Whisk together lemon juice, salt, and pepper in a large bowl, then add oil in a slow stream, whisking until combined.

▸ Arrange slices of *bresaola*, overlapping slightly, to cover a large platter. Drizzle all but ½ tablespoon vinaigrette over meat, then sprinkle generously with egg mixture.

▸ Add arugula and cheese to remaining vinaigrette in bowl and toss to coat lightly. Mound salad in center of platter.

# Octopus Salad

Serves **8** | Active time: **30 minutes** | Start to finish: **2 hours**

Salads like this one are found all over the southeastern Italian region of Puglia, almost always with carrot, celery, and parsley (a combination popular for its gorgeous color contrasts as well as its freshness and crunch) and lightly dressed with olive oil and lemon.

2 pounds frozen octopus, thawed and rinsed
⅓ cup chopped fresh flat-leaf parsley
3 garlic cloves, finely chopped
1 celery rib, halved lengthwise and thinly sliced crosswise
1 carrot, halved lengthwise and very thinly sliced crosswise
¼ cup extra-virgin olive oil
¼ cup fresh lemon juice
½ teaspoon black pepper
   Fine sea salt
¼ teaspoon dried oregano

▸ Cut off and discard head of octopus, then cut tentacles into 1-inch pieces. Generously cover octopus with water in a heavy medium pot and gently simmer, uncovered, until tender, 45 minutes to 1 hour.
▸ Drain octopus in a colander and cool to room temperature, then transfer to a bowl. Stir in remaining ingredients, and additional sea salt to taste.
▸ Let stand for 30 minutes for flavors to develop.

**COOKS' NOTE:** The octopus salad, without the parsley, can be made 1 day ahead and chilled, covered. Stir in the parsley just before serving.

KITCHEN TIP
**FROZEN ASSETS**

Octopus is the exception to the "fresh is better" rule. Frozen octopus cooks more quickly than fresh and is easier to find (though you may have to order from your fishmonger or supermarket a few days in advance). Don't be surprised if you are handed a solid frozen block; it will thaw in water into the recognizable cephalopod. We tested the Italian trick of tenderizing whole octopus by adding 2 wine corks to the boiling water, but it didn't seem to make any difference to cooking time or tenderness.

# Mushroom and Mozzarella Arancini

Makes **12 balls** | Active time: **30 minutes** | Start to finish: **30 minutes**

The Mushroom Risotto on page 76 is the basis for these delicious fried rice balls stuffed with melting chunks of mozzarella. Be sure your risotto is very well chilled, preferably overnight, so it's had a chance to firm up.

3  cups chilled Mushroom Risotto (see recipe, page 76)
12  (½-inch) cubes mozzarella (about 1 ounce total)
1  cup all-purpose flour
2  large eggs, lightly beaten
1  cup fine dry bread crumbs (not seasoned)
   About 8 cups vegetable oil for frying

**SPECIAL EQUIPMENT**
   **Deep-fat thermometer**

▶ Roll chilled risotto into 12 (1½-inch) balls using wet hands. Poke a small hole in center of each ball and insert a cube of cheese, then re-form into a ball.

▶ Put flour, eggs, and bread crumbs in three separate bowls. Dredge 1 ball in flour, shaking off excess. Dip in egg, letting excess drip off, then dredge in bread crumbs and transfer to a sheet of wax paper. Repeat with remaining balls.

▶ Heat 1½ to 2 inches oil in a 4- to 5-quart heavy pot until thermometer registers 360°F. Working in batches of 4, lower rice balls into oil with a slotted spoon and fry, turning occasionally, until golden brown, 2 to 3 minutes per batch. Transfer with slotted spoon to paper towels to drain. Return oil to 360°F between batches.

▶ Let balls stand for 2 minutes (for cheese to melt).

KITCHEN TIP
## ARANCINI MADE EASY

This is the type of recipe that will convince you it's worth taking the time to assemble all your ingredients—what the French call *mise en place*—before you begin. Have three separate small bowls ready to hold the coating ingredients—flour, beaten egg, and plain dry bread crumbs—as well as a baking sheet or tray lined with wax paper to hold the balls once they are coated. You'll also want a bowl of water to dip your hands into periodically when forming them. When it's time to coat the *arancini* (don't try to do more than one at a time), just use one hand so the other will be free of multiple layers of goopy coating to answer the phone or open the fridge.

< *Pizza Margherita, page 46*

**CHAPTER 2**

# PANINI & PIZZA

It makes sense that a country obsessed with bread would come up with what are arguably the world's most brilliant ways to eat it—as filled-and-pressed panini, or pizza crusts so crisp and chewy that a drizzle of olive oil and a sprinkling of herbs are all they need to become a perfect snack. The secret to great pizza and panini is in the dough, and we love making it from scratch. But fortunately, high-quality premade doughs and artisanal breads are now widely available on these shores, so even when time is tight, we can play freely with fillings and toppings that reflect the seasons and the whims of appetite: Taleggio and truffled mushrooms in fall, ripe tomatoes and fragrant basil in high summer, creamy Gorgonzola and caramelized onions any old time.

# Provolone and Broccoli Rabe Panini

Serves **2** | Active time: **20 minutes** | Start to finish: **20 minutes**

Sautéed broccoli rabe and melted provolone cheese are a hoagie combo made famous at Tony Luke's cheesesteak shop in Philadelphia—but you don't need to go that far to taste why it works!

½ **pound broccoli rabe, tough ends discarded**
2 **flat anchovies, rinsed, patted dry, and chopped**
1 **garlic clove, minced**
3 **tablespoons extra-virgin olive oil**
1 **(8- to 9-inch) sliced (¼-inch thick) fine-quality round Italian loaf**
⅓ **pound sliced provolone**

▶ Cook broccoli rabe in a 4-quart pot of well-salted boiling water, uncovered, until tender, about 3 minutes. Drain well in a colander, then chop.

▶ Cook anchovies and garlic in 1½ tablespoons oil in a 10-inch heavy skillet over medium heat, stirring, until garlic just begins to turn golden, about 1 minute. Add broccoli rabe and cook, stirring, 1 minute.

▶ Heat a panini or sandwich press according to manufacturer's instructions until hot. (Alternatively, heat a ridged grill pan over medium heat.)

▶ Brush 4 center slices of bread on 1 side with remaining 1½ tablespoons oil. (Reserve remainder of loaf for another use.) Put slices, oiled sides down, on a work surface, then divide half of cheese between 2 slices. Top with all of broccoli rabe mixture, remaining cheese, and remaining 2 bread slices, oiled sides up.

▶ Put sandwiches on press, then pull down top onto sandwiches and cook until browned and crisp, 4 to 8 minutes.

KITCHEN TIP
## TOASTING PANINI WITHOUT A PRESS

If you don't own an electric panini or sandwich press, simply put the sandwiches in a ridged grill pan or cast-iron skillet, and weight them down with another heavy pan. Flip them over halfway through cooking, and in less than 10 minutes, they'll be pressed and browned.

# Torta al Testo

Flatbread Stuffed with Cheese and Prosciutto
*Adapted from Ursula Ferrigno*

**Serves 2 to 4 | Active time: 45 minutes | Start to finish: 2 hours**

This unorthodox *panino*—you work in reverse, griddling the bread first, then layering it with prosciutto, Fontina, and arugula before baking—results in a warm, gooey flatbread with a crunchy crust.

1⅛ teaspoon active dry yeast
⅔ cup warm water (105–115°F)
9 ounces unbleached bread flour
   (about 1¾ cups plus 2 tablespoons)
   Salt
½ tablespoon olive oil
¼ pound thinly sliced Italian Fontina,
   Gruyère, or Emmental cheese
2 cups baby arugula
6 thin prosciutto slices
   Black pepper

▶ Stir together yeast and ⅓ cup warm water in a small bowl and let stand until foamy, about 5 minutes. (If mixture doesn't foam, start over with new yeast.)
▶ Stir together flour and ¾ teaspoon salt with a fork in a large bowl. Make a well in center and add yeast mixture and oil. Stir in flour, then stir in as much of remaining ⅓ cup water as needed to form a firm, moist dough.
▶ Turn dough out onto a lightly floured surface and knead until smooth, shiny, and elastic, about 10 minutes.
▶ Put dough in cleaned large bowl and cover bowl. Let rise in a draft-free place at warm room temperature until doubled, about 1 hour.
▶ Punch down dough and halve. Form each piece into a ball and let stand, covered, 10 minutes.

▶ Roll out each ball on a lightly floured surface with a rolling pin into an 8-inch round (about ¼-inch thick; if dough resists, let stand for 1 to 2 minutes, then continue).
▶ Preheat oven to 400°F, with rack in middle.
▶ Heat a heavy medium skillet or griddle over medium-low heat until very hot, about 10 minutes. Cook rounds 1 at a time, flipping frequently to avoid scorching, until golden, about 6 minutes per round; stack and wrap in a towel (not terry cloth).
▶ When rounds are cool, separate into halves by cutting into bread all around edge and gently pulling rounds apart. Sandwich cheese, arugula, prosciutto, and salt and pepper to taste between halves.
▶ Put stuffed breads on a baking sheet and bake until crisp and cheese has melted, about 8 minutes. Cut into wedges and serve warm.

**COOKS' NOTE:** The unstuffed loaves can be cooked 2 hours ahead and kept in a towel.

# Caramelized-Onion and Gorgonzola Grilled Pizza

Serves **4** | Active time: **30 minutes** | Start to finish: **40 minutes**

When the alluringly charred crust of a grilled pizza is topped with ingredients that have a natural affinity for one another—sweet cooked-down onions, toasted walnuts, and mild, creamy Gorgonzola *dolce*—you've got an irresistible winner.

- 6 tablespoons extra-virgin olive oil
- 1¼ pounds onions (2 large), halved lengthwise and thinly sliced
- ½ teaspoon salt
- ¼ teaspoon black pepper
- 1 pound pizza dough, thawed completely if frozen
- ¼ pound Gorgonzola *dolce*, crumbled (1 cup)
- ½ cup walnuts, toasted and coarsely chopped
- ¼ cup chopped fresh flat-leaf parsley

▶ Heat ¼ cup oil in a 12-inch heavy skillet over medium-low heat until it shimmers, then cook onions with salt and pepper, covered, stirring occasionally, until golden, 15 to 20 minutes. Transfer to a small bowl and keep warm, covered.

▶ Prepare a grill for direct-heat cooking over low charcoal (medium heat for gas); see instructions on page 11.

▶ Stretch dough into a roughly 12-by-10-inch rectangle on a large baking sheet and brush with 1 tablespoon oil.

▶ Bring dough, onions, cheese, nuts, parsley, and remaining tablespoon oil to grill area.

▶ Oil grill rack, then put dough, oiled side down, on grill and brush top with remaining tablespoon oil. Grill, covered, until underside is golden brown, 1½ to 3 minutes.

▶ Using tongs, return crust to baking sheet, turning crust over (grilled side up). Sprinkle evenly with onions, cheese, nuts, and parsley. Slide pizza from sheet onto grill and grill, covered, until underside is golden brown and cheese is partially melted, about 3 minutes. Transfer to a cutting board and cut into pieces.

**COOKS' NOTES:** The onions can be cooked 1 day ahead and chilled.

The nuts can be toasted 1 day ahead and cooled, then kept in an airtight container at room temperature.

# Truffled Taleggio and Mushroom Pizza

Serves **4** | Active time: **10 minutes** | Start to finish: **30 minutes**

Four ingredients and a few minutes are all it takes to put together this crisp, bubbly masterpiece. A quick drizzle of truffle oil adds a final decadent flourish. You may never order in again.

1  **pound pizza dough, thawed completely if frozen**
½  **pound sliced mushrooms**
   **Salt and pepper**
¾  **pound cold Taleggio or Italian Fontina, rind discarded and cheese sliced**
1  **teaspoon white truffle oil (optional)**

**SPECIAL EQUIPMENT**
   **17-by-14-inch sheet of parchment paper**

▶ Put a large heavy baking sheet (17 by 14 inches) on lowest rack of oven, then preheat oven to 500°F.

▶ Stretch out dough on a lightly floured surface, pulling on corners to form a roughly 16-by-13-inch rectangle. (Dough will be easier to stretch as it warms.) Transfer to a large tray lined with parchment paper. Lightly prick dough all over with a fork.

▶ Slide dough (still on parchment) onto hot baking sheet. Bake until top is puffed and pale golden in patches, 6 to 10 minutes.

▶ Remove from oven; prick any large bubbles with a fork and flatten. Scatter mushrooms over crust, then season with salt and pepper and lay cheese on top.

▶ Bake pizza until edge of crust is deep golden and cheese is bubbling and golden in patches, 8 to 10 minutes. Drizzle with truffle oil (if using) and season with pepper. Serve immediately.

# Three-Cheese Pizza with Onion, Sage, and Arugula

**Serves 4** | **Active time: 45 minutes** | **Start to finish: 2¼ hours**

Why a trio of cheeses? Fontina for its melting quality and nutty flavor, Gorgonzola for its biting blue punch, and Parmigiano-Reggiano for its uncanny ability to amplify other cheeses.

Pizza Dough (page 171), shaped into a ball and allowed to rise

- 1 tablespoon extra-virgin olive oil
- ¼ pound Italian Fontina, cut into ½-inch pieces
- 2 ounces Gorgonzola *dolce*, cut into ¼-inch pieces
- ½ cup thinly sliced red onion
- 6 large fresh sage leaves, thinly sliced crosswise (1 tablespoon)
- ¼ cup grated Parmigiano-Reggiano
- 4 ounces baby arugula leaves (6 cups)

**SPECIAL EQUIPMENT**
Pizza stone

▶ **HEAT PIZZA STONE WHILE DOUGH RISES:** At least 45 minutes before baking pizza, put stone in lower third of an electric oven (or on floor of gas oven) and preheat oven to 500°F. Line a pizza peel or large baking sheet (without sides) with parchment paper.

▶ **SHAPE DOUGH:** Do not punch down. Dust dough with flour, then transfer to lined pizza peel or baking sheet. Pat out dough evenly with your fingers and stretch into a 14-inch round, reflouring fingers if necessary.

▶ **ASSEMBLE PIZZA:** Brush dough with oil, leaving a 1-inch border, then scatter Fontina and Gorgonzola over dough (leaving a 1-inch border). Scatter onion and sage over cheese and sprinkle pizza with Parmigiano-Reggiano. Slide pizza on parchment onto pizza stone. Bake until dough is crisp and browned and cheese is bubbling, 10 to 15 minutes. Slide peel or baking sheet under parchment to remove pizza from oven, then transfer to a cutting board. Top with arugula.

**COOKS' NOTE:** If you don't have time to make your own pizza dough, you can make a delicious pizza with 1 pound store-bought dough.

**KITCHEN TIP**
## PIZZA WITHOUT TEARS

Sometimes the simplest tool can make a profound difference. Take parchment paper and pizza. If you use a pizza stone—which really is worth the investment—the classic method is to dust the pizza peel (that paddle used for sliding pizza around) with cornmeal so that the dough will slide smoothly onto the super-hot stone. Trust us, it's not easy; it takes a lot of practice, and inevitably there are disasters. But if you line a baking sheet or peel with parchment first, then pat out the dough on it and slide the parchment onto the stone, you will be amazed at how smooth the process becomes. Suddenly, pizza is ridiculously easy; no more catastrophes.

# Pizza with Fontina, Prosciutto, and Arugula

**Serves 4** | **Active time: 10 minutes** | Start to finish: **30 minutes**

No time to heat up a pizza stone? This easy alternative method yields a crisp crust in just minutes. Good cheese, olive oil, and prosciutto go a long way toward making the pie truly memorable.

1 **pound pizza dough, thawed completely if frozen**
¾ **pound well-chilled Italian Fontina (see Cooks' Note), any rind discarded**
1 **garlic clove, forced through a garlic press**
4 **ounces baby arugula (6 cups)**
¼ **pound thinly sliced prosciutto**
   **Extra-virgin olive oil for drizzling**
   **Freshly ground black pepper**

**SPECIAL EQUIPMENT**
   **17-by-14-inch sheet of parchment paper**

▶ Put a large heavy baking sheet (17 by 14 inches) on lowest rack of oven, then preheat oven to 500°F.

▶ Meanwhile, stretch out dough on a lightly floured surface, pulling on corners to form a 16-by-13-inch rectangle. (Dough will be easier to stretch as it warms.) Transfer to a large tray lined with parchment paper. Lightly prick dough all over with a fork, then slide dough (on parchment) from tray onto hot baking sheet. Bake until top is puffed and pale golden in patches, 6 to 10 minutes.

▶ While crust bakes, shred cheese in a food processor fitted with medium shredding disk (you should have 3 cups).

▶ Remove crust from oven; prick any large bubbles with a fork and flatten. Brush all over with crushed garlic, then sprinkle evenly with cheese. Bake pizza until edge of crust is deep golden and cheese is bubbling and golden in patches, 8 to 10 minutes.

▶ Remove from oven, then scatter arugula over pizza and drape prosciutto over arugula. Drizzle with oil and coarsely ground pepper to taste. Serve immediately.

**COOKS' NOTE:** In place of the Fontina, you can use 1 pound smoked mozzarella, cut into ¼-inch-thick slices.

# Pizza Margherita

**Serves 4 | Active time: 1 hour | Start to finish: 2¼ hours**

The secret to a great pizza Margherita is to use the best ingredients you can find—with a degree of restraint. (Just because a little cheese is good doesn't mean a lot will be better.) We always start with our favorite dough (see page 171), adapted from chef Chris Bianco, of Pizzeria Bianco, in Phoenix.

Pizza Dough (page 171), shaped into a ball and allowed to rise
1  (14- to 15-ounce) can whole tomatoes in juice
2  large garlic cloves, smashed
2  tablespoons olive oil
4  basil leaves, plus more for sprinkling
¼  teaspoon sugar
   Salt
6  ounces fresh mozzarella, cut into ¼-inch-thick slices

**SPECIAL EQUIPMENT**
   Pizza stone

▶ **MAKE TOMATO SAUCE WHILE DOUGH RISES:** Pulse tomatoes with juice in a blender briefly to make a chunky puree. Cook garlic in oil in a small heavy saucepan over medium-low heat, stirring, until fragrant and pale golden, about 2 minutes. Add tomato puree, basil, sugar, and ⅛ teaspoon salt and simmer, uncovered, stirring occasionally, until thickened and reduced to about 1 cup, 30 to 40 minutes. Season with salt and cool.

▶ **HEAT PIZZA STONE WHILE MAKING TOMATO SAUCE:** At least 45 minutes before baking pizza, put stone on oven rack in lower third of electric oven (or on floor of gas oven) and preheat oven to 500°F. Line a pizza peel or large baking sheet without sides with parchment.

▶ **SHAPE DOUGH:** Do not punch down. Dust dough with flour, then transfer to lined pizza peel or baking sheet. Pat out dough evenly with your fingers and stretch into a 14-inch round, reflouring fingers if necessary.

▶ **ASSEMBLE PIZZA:** Spread sauce over dough, leaving a 1-inch border (there may be some sauce left over). Arrange cheese on top, leaving a 2- to 3-inch border.

▶ Slide pizza on parchment onto pizza stone. Bake until dough is crisp and browned and cheese is golden and bubbling in spots, 12 to 16 minutes. Slide peel or baking sheet under parchment to remove pizza from oven, then transfer to a cutting board. Cool for 5 minutes. Sprinkle with some basil leaves before slicing.

**COOKS' NOTES:** The tomato sauce can be made 5 days ahead and chilled.

If you don't have time to make your own pizza dough, you can make a delicious pizza with 1 pound store-bought dough.

< *Cacio e Pepe, page 52*

**CHAPTER 3**

# PASTA, POLENTA & RISOTTO

Italophiles may gently point out that we Americans don't eat pasta properly, that it's meant to be a small, lightly sauced course. But with all due respect, we can't help ourselves! Pasta and risotto are so simple to cook on a busy weeknight, and so utterly satisfying to eat any time at all, that we wind up making them the main event of meal after meal: linguine tangled up with boatloads of clams, risotto suffused with wild mushrooms, manicotti rolled around a luscious three-cheese filling. Not to say that we don't appreciate the allure of a perfect strand of fresh pasta in all its near-naked glory. Only that we also admire it piled high on a platter, smothered with meatballs, and accompanied by nothing other than a glass of wine and a fresh green salad.

# Pasta with Lentils and Kale

Serves **4** | Active time: **40 minutes** | Start to finish: **50 minutes**

The secret to this dish is the caramelized onions: Cook them long and slow until they are meltingly tender and golden brown. Their rich sweetness rounds out the earthiness of the lentils and kale.

**KITCHEN TIP**

## TOASTED CRUMBS FOR PASTA

Sprinkle these on anything for an addictive hit of salty crunch. The better the bread you use, the better the crumbs. Sourdough works particularly well. (It's a great way to use up the heels of your loaves; freeze them and when you've got a good pile, make crumbs.) Slice the bread and cut it into roughly 1-inch pieces. Coarsely grind the bread into crumbs in a blender (it works well in small batches) or pulse all together in a food processor. Spread out the crumbs on a baking sheet and bake in a preheated 350°F oven, stirring once or twice, until golden, 10 to 15 minutes. Pour them into a bowl, and for every cup of crumbs, drizzle with 1½ to 2 table-spoons extra-virgin olive oil, or to taste, and toss well. Season the crumbs with salt.

½ cup French (small) green lentils

2 cups water

Salt

5 tablespoons extra-virgin olive oil

2 medium onions, finely chopped (2 cups)

Black pepper

¾ pound kale, preferably Tuscan

¾ pound dried short tubular pasta

ACCOMPANIMENTS

Toasted Crumbs for Pasta (see Kitchen Tip) and/or grated Parmigiano-Reggiano

▶ Simmer lentils in water (2 cups) with ⅛ teaspoon salt in a small saucepan, uncovered, adding more water if necessary to keep lentils barely covered, until tender but not falling apart, 20 to 30 minutes. Remove from heat and season with salt.

▶ While lentils simmer, heat 3 tablespoons oil in a 12-inch heavy skillet over medium-high heat until it shimmers, then sauté onion with ¼ teaspoon salt and ½ teaspoon pepper, stirring, 1 minute. Reduce heat to low and cook, covered, stirring occasionally, until onions are soft and golden (stir more frequently toward end of cooking), about 20 minutes. Remove lid and increase heat to medium, then cook, stirring frequently, until onions are golden brown, 5 to 10 minutes more. Stir in lentils, including their liquid, and simmer, scraping up any brown bits, 1 minute. Season with salt and pepper.

▶ While onion cooks, cut out and discard stems and center ribs from kale and coarsely chop leaves. Start cooking pasta in a 6- to 8-quart pot of well-salted boiling water, according to package instructions.

▶ About 7 minutes before pasta is finished cooking, stir in kale and boil, uncovered, until pasta is al dente. Reserve about 1 cup cooking liquid, then drain pasta and kale in a colander. Add pasta mixture to lentils along with about ⅓ cup of cooking liquid (or enough to keep pasta moist) and cook over medium-high heat, tossing, 1 minute. Season with salt and pepper and drizzle with remaining 2 tablespoons oil. Sprinkle with toasted crumbs and/or cheese.

**COOKS' NOTES:** The lentils and onions can be cooked and combined up to 5 days ahead and chilled. Reheat over low heat, thinning with water as necessary.

The kale can be washed and trimmed 1 day ahead and chilled in a sealed plastic bag lined with dampened paper towels.

Tuscan kale is often labeled *lacinato* or dinosaur kale.

# Cacio e Pepe

Spaghetti with Pecorino Romano and Black Pepper

**Serves 2** | **Active time: 20 minutes** | **Start to finish: 20 minutes**

For a dish this straightforward, the ingredients must be absolutely stellar: true Pecorino Romano (if you can only find the pregrated supermarket stuff, use good-quality Parmigiano instead); durum wheat semolina spaghetti; toasted black peppercorns. Perfection on a plate!

2   teaspoons black peppercorns
½   pound spaghetti
¾   cup plus 2 tablespoons very finely grated Pecorino Romano

▶ Toast peppercorns in a dry small skillet over medium-high heat, swirling skillet, until fragrant and peppercorns begin to jump, 2 to 3 minutes. Coarsely crush peppercorns with a mortar and pestle or wrap in a kitchen towel and press with bottom of a heavy skillet.

▶ Cook spaghetti in a 6- to 8-quart pot of well-salted boiling water until al dente.

▶ Fill a large glass or ceramic bowl with some hot water to warm bowl. Just before spaghetti is finished cooking, drain bowl but do not dry.

▶ Reserve ½ cup cooking water, then drain pasta quickly in a colander (do not shake off excess water) and add to warm pasta bowl. Sprinkle ¾ cup cheese and 3 tablespoons cooking water evenly over spaghetti and toss quickly. If pasta seems dry, toss with some additional cooking water.

▶ Divide pasta between two plates, then sprinkle with pepper and 2 tablespoons cheese (total). Serve immediately with additional cheese on the side.

**COOKS' NOTE:** To prevent the cheese from clumping up in the bowl, grate it with the ragged-edged holes of a box grater, not a Microplane.

# Manicotti

Serves **6** | Active time: **1¼ hours** | Start to finish: **2 hours**

Unlike cannelloni, the egg pasta rolls with which they're frequently confused, manicotti are made from Italian-style crepes called *crespelle,* which you brown on one side and then wrap around a creamy three-cheese filling.

- 3 tablespoons olive oil
- 1 medium onion, chopped
- 3 garlic cloves, minced
- 2 (28-ounce) cans whole tomatoes in juice (preferably Italian), drained, reserving juice, and finely chopped
- ½ cup water
- 1 teaspoon sugar
- 1 teaspoon salt
- ¼ cup chopped fresh basil

**FOR CREPES**
- 3 large eggs
- 1½ cups water
- 1¼ cups all-purpose flour
- ½ teaspoon salt
- 1 tablespoon unsalted butter, melted

**FOR FILLING**
- 2 pounds fresh ricotta (3 cups)
- 2 large eggs
- ½ cup grated Parmigiano-Reggiano
- ⅓ cup chopped fresh parsley
- ½ teaspoon salt
- ½ teaspoon black pepper
- ½ pound fresh mozzarella

**SPECIAL EQUIPMENT**
- 2 glass or ceramic baking dishes, one 13 by 9 inches and one 8 inch square

▶ **MAKE SAUCE:** Heat oil in a 5- to 6-quart heavy pot over medium-high heat until it shimmers, then sauté onion until golden, about 6 minutes. Add garlic and sauté until golden, about 1 minute. Add tomatoes with juice, water, sugar, and salt and simmer, uncovered, stirring occasionally, until thickened, about 30 minutes. Stir in basil and remove from heat.

▶ **MAKE CREPES:** Break up eggs with a wooden spoon in a medium bowl and stir in water until combined (don't beat). Sift in flour and salt, then stir batter until just combined. Force through a medium-mesh sieve into another bowl.

▶ Lightly brush an 8-inch nonstick skillet with melted butter and heat over medium heat until hot. Ladle about ¼ cup batter into skillet, tilting and rotating skillet to coat bottom, then pour excess back into bowl. (If batter sets before skillet is coated, reduce heat slightly for next crepe.) Cook until underside is just set and lightly browned, about 30 seconds, then invert crepe onto a clean kitchen towel to cool completely. (Crepe is cooked on only one side.) Make at least 11 more crepes, brushing skillet with butter as needed and stacking crepes in 3 piles.

▶ **MAKE FILLING AND ASSEMBLE MANICOTTI:** Stir together ricotta, eggs, Parmigiano-Reggiano, parsley, salt, and pepper.

▶ Preheat oven to 425°F, with rack in middle.

▶ Cut mozzarella lengthwise into ¼-inch-thick sticks. Spread 2 cups sauce in larger baking dish and 1 cup in smaller one.

▶ Arrange 1 crepe, browned side up, on a work surface, then spread about ¼ cup filling in a line across center and top with a mozzarella strip. Fold in top and bottom to enclose filling, leaving ends open, and transfer, seam side down, to either baking dish. Fill 11 more crepes, arranging snugly in one layer in both dishes (8 in larger dish and 4 in smaller).

▶ Spread 1 cup sauce over manicotti in larger dish and ½ cup in smaller dish. Tightly cover dishes with foil and bake until sauce is bubbling and filling is hot, 15 to 20 minutes. Serve remaining sauce on the side.

**COOKS' NOTE:** The manicotti can be assembled (but not baked) 1 day ahead and chilled, covered with foil. Chill the remaining sauce, covered, separately. Let stand at room temperature for 15 minutes before baking, covered with foil. Reheat the sauce, thinning slightly with water.

# Linguine with White Clam Sauce

Serves **4** | Active time: **25 minutes** | Start to finish: **35 minutes**

Although they're not technically clams, cockles work best in this classic dish, since they're very small and have delicate, sweet flesh. You can identify them by their tiny size (about ½ to 1 inch across) and green-tinged shells.

⅓ cup extra-virgin olive oil
1 medium onion, chopped
6 garlic cloves, finely chopped
¾ teaspoon hot red-pepper flakes
¼ teaspoon dried oregano
⅓ cup dry white wine
⅓ cup bottled clam juice
1 pound linguine
2 pounds small cockles (up to 1 inch across; 5–6 dozen), scrubbed well
2 tablespoons cold unsalted butter, cut into small pieces
⅓ cup chopped fresh flat-leaf parsley
Salt

**ACCOMPANIMENTS**
Extra-virgin olive oil for drizzling, hot red-pepper flakes

**KITCHEN TIP**
## THE RIGHT AMOUNT OF SALT FOR PASTA WATER

You don't need oil in your pasta-cooking water, but you do—desperately—need salt. The old rule of thumb is that the water should taste of the sea, so don't be timid: 2 tablespoons salt per 4 quarts water. Also remember to give the pasta plenty of room; use at least 5 quarts of water per pound of pasta.

▶ Heat oil in a 5- to 6-quart heavy pot over medium-high heat until it shimmers, then sauté onion until golden, about 4 minutes. Add garlic, red-pepper flakes, and oregano and sauté until garlic is golden, about 2 minutes. Stir in wine and clam juice and boil, uncovered, stirring occasionally, until slightly reduced, about 3 minutes.

▶ Cook pasta in a 6- to 8-quart pot of well-salted boiling water until al dente, then drain in a colander.

▶ While pasta is cooking, stir cockles into sauce and simmer, covered, stirring occasionally, until cockles open wide, 4 to 6 minutes. (Discard any cockles that have not opened after 6 minutes.) Remove from heat and stir in butter until melted.

▶ Add pasta to cockles along with parsley and salt to taste, then toss well. Serve and pass around the olive oil and red-pepper flakes.

# Capellini with Shrimp and Creamy Tomato Sauce

Serves **4** | Active time: **10 minutes** | Start to finish: **15 minutes**

The sweet vermouth punctuates the natural sweetness of the canned tomatoes, making this quick sauce so lush and velvety, it tastes as if it has been simmered for hours.

3  tablespoons olive oil
1  pound peeled large shrimp
3  large garlic cloves, forced through a garlic press
¼  teaspoon dried oregano
½  teaspoon salt
¼  teaspoon black pepper
½  cup sweet (red) vermouth
1  (14- to 15-ounce) can diced tomatoes, drained
¾  cup heavy cream
½  teaspoon fresh lemon juice
½  pound capellini (angel-hair pasta)

▶ Heat oil in a 12-inch heavy skillet over medium-high heat until it shimmers, then cook shrimp and garlic with oregano, salt, and pepper, turning once, until golden, about 2 minutes total. Stir in vermouth and tomatoes, scraping up any brown bits from bottom of skillet. Add cream and briskly simmer until sauce has thickened slightly, about 1 minute. Stir in lemon juice.

▶ Meanwhile, cook capellini in a 6- to 8-quart pot of well-salted boiling water until al dente. Reserve 1 cup cooking water, then drain pasta.

▶ Serve immediately, topped with shrimp and sauce. Thin sauce with some reserved cooking water if necessary.

# Spaghetti and Meatballs

**Serves 12 to 16** | Active time: **2 hours** | Start to finish: **3 hours**

The stars of this dish are the meatballs, and they don't disappoint—lots of garlic and Parmigiano-Reggiano give them a robustness that stands up to the hearty tomato sauce. If you're not cooking for a crowd, you can freeze the leftovers with the sauce for more joy another day.

- 6 (28-ounce) cans whole tomatoes in juice (preferably San Marzano)
- 2 medium onions, chopped
- ½ cup extra-virgin olive oil
- 6 garlic cloves, finely chopped
- 4 teaspoons salt, plus more to taste
- 1 teaspoon black pepper

**FOR MEATBALLS**
- 2 medium onions, finely chopped
- ¼ cup extra-virgin olive oil
- 10 garlic cloves, finely chopped
- 3 cups torn day-old Italian bread
- 3 cups whole milk
- 6 large eggs
- 2 cups grated Parmigiano-Reggiano (¼ pound)
- ⅓ cup finely chopped fresh flat-leaf parsley
- ¼ cup finely chopped fresh oregano or 1 teaspoon dried, crumbled
- 1 tablespoon grated lemon zest
- 5½ teaspoons salt
- 1½ teaspoons black pepper
- 1½ pounds ground veal
- 1½ pounds ground pork
- 1½ pounds ground beef (not lean)
- 1 cup olive or vegetable oil

**FOR PASTA**
- 2 pounds dried spaghetti

**ACCOMPANIMENT**
- Grated Parmigiano-Reggiano

**SPECIAL EQUIPMENT**
- 12- to 16-quart nonreactive heavy pot or two smaller nonreactive pots, 6- to 8-quart pot with a pasta/steamer insert

**KITCHEN TIP**
## MEATBALL MIX

You'll often see ground beef, pork, and veal packaged as "meatball mix" or "meat-loaf mix" at the grocery store, but if the meats have already been blended, avoid buying them. Too fine a grind is often used when they are processed together, so the finished meatballs or loaf will likely be tough, not tender. And if you can't find the veal, don't worry about it: Beef and pork alone also yield great results. Another rule of thumb: Don't buy lean ground beef or pork, since their lack of fat will make the meatballs less moist.

▶ **MAKE SAUCE:** Drain tomatoes, reserving juice in a large bowl. Crush tomatoes with your hands and add to juice.

▶ Cook onions in oil in pot over medium heat, stirring occasionally, until softened. Add garlic and cook, stirring occasionally, until softened, about 2 minutes. Stir in tomatoes with their juice, salt, and pepper. Simmer, uncovered, stirring occasionally, until slightly thickened, 45 minutes to 1 hour. Season with salt.

▶ **MAKE MEATBALLS WHILE SAUCE SIMMERS:** Cook onions in extra-virgin olive oil in a 12-inch heavy skillet over medium heat, stirring occasionally, until softened, about 10 minutes. Add garlic and cook, stirring occasionally, until softened, about 3 minutes. Transfer to a large bowl to cool.

▶ Soak bread in milk in another bowl until soft, about 5 minutes. Squeeze bread to remove excess milk, discarding milk.

▶ Stir together onion mixture, bread, eggs, Parmesan, parsley, oregano, zest, salt, and pepper until combined. Add meats to bread mixture, gently mixing with your hands until just combined (do not overmix).

▶ Form mixture into about 70 (1½-inch) balls with dampened hands, arranging on two large baking sheets.

▶ Heat olive or vegetable oil (1 cup) in a 12-inch heavy skillet over medium-high heat until it shimmers, then brown meatballs in 4 or 5 small batches, turning fre-

quently, about 5 minutes per batch. Transfer to a clean large bowl.

▶ Add meatballs to sauce and gently simmer, covered, stirring occasionally, until cooked through, 20 to 30 minutes. (If necessary, divide mixture between two pots.)

▶ **PREPARE PASTA:** Cook spaghetti in 2 batches in pasta insert in well-salted boiling water until al dente, draining and tossing each batch with some of sauce in a large serving dish.

▶ Serve with meatballs, remaining sauce, and grated cheese.

# Sunday Ragù

It looks like plain tomato sauce, but this thick, intense *ragù* is enriched with beef *braciole,* Italian sausage, and pork. Traditionally the pasta—tossed with just enough sauce to coat the noodles—is served before the platter of meat. This dish takes time but is well worth waiting for.

Serves **12** | Active time: **1¼ hours** | Start to finish: **4 hours**

5 (28-ounce) cans whole tomatoes in juice (preferably Italian)
½ cup olive oil
1 large onion, finely chopped
5 garlic cloves, minced
1 Turkish bay leaf or ½ California
½ teaspoon salt

**FOR BEEF BRACIOLE**

4 garlic cloves, minced
½ cup finely chopped fresh flat-leaf parsley
1 cup grated Pecorino Romano (2 ounces)
3 ounces thinly sliced pancetta, finely chopped
1½ pounds beef top round, cut across the grain into ¼-inch slices
¾ teaspoon salt
½ teaspoon black pepper

**FOR OTHER MEATS**

½ cup olive oil for frying
1 pound sweet Italian sausage links
1 pound hot Italian sausage links
1½ pounds boneless pork shoulder, cut into 2-inch pieces
¾ teaspoon salt
½ teaspoon black pepper
2 pounds country-style pork ribs

**SPECIAL EQUIPMENT**

Kitchen string

**ACCOMPANIMENT**

Fresh Egg Fettuccine (page 169) or 1¼ pounds dried egg fettuccine

▶ **MAKE TOMATO SAUCE:** Pulse tomatoes with juice (one can at a time) in a blender until almost smooth.

breaking up any lumps, until meat is no longer pink, 6 to 10 minutes. Stir in wine, milk, tomato paste, thyme, salt, and pepper. Simmer, uncovered, stirring occasionally, until most of liquid has evaporated but sauce is still moist, about 1 hour.

▶ **MAKE RICOTTA FILLING:** Put spinach in a kitchen towel (not terry cloth) and twist to squeeze out as much moisture as possible.

▶ Whisk together ricotta, eggs, Parmesan, nutmeg, salt, and pepper. Transfer 1½ cups ricotta mixture to another bowl and whisk in ¼ cup milk; set aside. Whisk spinach into remaining filling with remaining ½ cup milk.

▶ **ASSEMBLE AND BAKE LASAGNE:** Preheat oven to 375°F, with rack in middle.

▶ Soak noodles in a bowl of very warm water until pliable but not softened, 3 to 5 minutes. Place on a kitchen towel (it's not necessary to pat noodles dry).

▶ Spread 1½ cups Bolognese sauce in baking pan and sprinkle with 1 tablespoon Parmesan. Cover with 3 noodles, leaving space in between. Spread half of spinach filling on top, then 1 cup Bolognese sauce, and top with 1 tablespoon Parmesan and 3 noodles; repeat. Top with remaining Bolognese sauce, 1 tablespoon Parmesan, and remaining 3 noodles. Pour reserved ricotta mixture over top and sprinkle with remaining ¼ cup Parmesan.

▶ Cover pan tightly with parchment paper and foil (or just buttered foil) and bake 50 minutes. Remove foil and bake until top is browned in spots, about 15 minutes more. Let stand for 15 to 30 minutes before cutting.

**COOKS' NOTES:** The Bolognese sauce can be made 2 days ahead and chilled (covered once cool).

The lasagne can be made 1 day ahead and chilled. Reheat in a 350°F oven, loosely covered with foil.

# Sweet Potato Gnocchi with Fried Sage and Chestnuts

When tender orange gnocchi are topped with crisp sage leaves and chestnuts, you've got a real wow dish. Making these ridged dumplings takes practice, but don't worry about perfection: You're just adding a little roughness to give the sauce something to cling to.

Serves **6** | Active time: **1¼ hours** | Start to finish: **2¼ hours**

- 1¼ **pounds russet (baking) potatoes**
- 1 **(¾-pound) sweet potato**
- 1 **large egg**
- ½ **teaspoon freshly grated nutmeg**
- **Salt**
- ½ **teaspoon black pepper**
- ⅓ **cup grated Parmigiano-Reggiano, plus more for serving**
- 1½–2 **cups all-purpose flour**
- ⅓ **cup extra-virgin olive oil**
- 1 **cup sage leaves (from 1 bunch)**
- ⅓ **cup bottled roasted chestnuts, very thinly sliced with an adjustable-blade slicer or a sharp vegetable peeler**
- 2 **tablespoons unsalted butter**

**SPECIAL EQUIPMENT**
**Potato ricer or food mill fitted with fine disk**

▶ Preheat oven to 450°F, with rack in middle.

▶ Pierce russet and sweet potatoes in several places with a fork, then bake on a baking sheet until just tender, 45 minutes to 1 hour.

▶ Cool potatoes slightly, then peel and force through ricer onto baking sheet, spreading in an even layer. Cool potatoes completely.

▶ Lightly flour two or three large baking sheets or line with parchment paper.

▶ Beat together egg, nutmeg, 1 teaspoon salt, and the pepper in a small bowl.

▶ Gather potatoes into a mound on baking sheet, and form a well in center.

▶ Pour egg mixture into well, then knead into potatoes. Knead in cheese and 1½ cups flour, then knead, adding more flour as necessary, until mixture forms a smooth but slightly sticky dough. Dust top lightly with flour.

▶ Cut dough into 6 pieces. Form 1 piece of dough into a ½-inch-thick rope on a lightly floured surface. Cut rope into ½-inch pieces. Gently roll each piece into a ball and lightly dust with flour.

▶ Repeat with remaining dough.

▶ Turn a fork over and hold at a 45-degree angle, with tips of tines touching work surface. Working with one at a time, roll gnocchi down fork tines, pressing with your thumb, to make ridges on one side; transfer as formed to baking sheets.

▶ **FRY SAGE LEAVES AND CHESTNUTS:** Heat oil in a 12-inch heavy skillet over medium heat until it shimmers. Fry sage leaves in 3 batches, stirring, until they turn just a shade lighter and crisp (they will continue to crisp as they cool), about 30 seconds per batch. Transfer to paper towels to drain. Season lightly with salt.

▶ Fry chestnuts in 3 batches, stirring, until golden and crisp, about 30 seconds per batch. Transfer to paper towels to drain. Season lightly with salt. Reserve oil in skillet.

▶ **MAKE SAUCE:** Add butter to oil in skillet with ½ teaspoon salt and cook until golden brown, 1 to 2 minutes. Remove from heat.

▶ **COOK GNOCCHI:** Add half of gnocchi to a 6- to 8-quart pot of well-salted boiling water and stir. Cook until they float to surface, about 3 minutes. Transfer with a slotted spoon to skillet with butter sauce. Cook remaining gnocchi, transferring to skillet as cooked.

▶ Heat gnocchi in skillet over medium heat, stirring to coat.

▶ Serve sprinkled with fried sage and chestnuts and additional grated cheese.

**COOKS' NOTE:** The uncooked gnocchi can be frozen (first in one layer on a baking sheet, then transferred to a sealable bag) up to 1 month. Do not thaw before cooking.

# Souffléed Gnocchi

Serves **6** | Active time: **35 minutes** | Start to finish: **2 hours**

One bite of these Roman-style gnocchi, made with semolina flour, and you'll be smitten with their cheesy, pillow-soft tenderness.

3 **cups whole milk**

¾ **teaspoon salt**

¾ **cup semolina (3 ounces; sometimes labeled "semolina flour")**

3 **large eggs**

7 **tablespoons grated Parmigiano-Reggiano**

4½ **tablespoons unsalted butter, softened**

**SPECIAL EQUIPMENT**
  **2-inch round cookie cutter;**
  **2-quart shallow baking dish**

▶ Bring milk with the salt to a simmer in a 2- to 3-quart heavy saucepan over medium-low heat. Add semolina in a slow stream, whisking, then simmer, stirring constantly with a wooden spoon, 12 minutes (mixture will be very stiff). Remove from heat and stir in eggs 1 at a time, then stir in 6 tablespoons cheese and 3 tablespoons butter. Spread into a ½-inch-thick slab on an oiled baking sheet using a lightly oiled rubber spatula, then chill, uncovered, until cool to the touch, about 10 minutes.

▶ Cut out rounds from gnocchi with cookie cutter dipped in cool water (incorporating scraps as you work) and gently transfer rounds (they will be very soft), slightly overlapping, to buttered baking dish. Chill gnocchi, uncovered, for 1 hour.

▶ Preheat oven to 450°F, with racks in upper and lower thirds.

▶ Melt remaining 1½ tablespoons butter and brush over gnocchi, then sprinkle with remaining tablespoon cheese. Bake in upper third of oven for 10 minutes, then switch dish to lower third of oven and continue to bake until gnocchi are slightly puffed and lightly browned, about 10 minutes more. Let stand for 5 minutes before serving.

**COOKS' NOTE:** The unbaked gnocchi can be chilled up to 1 day, covered after 1 hour.

# Creamy White Polenta with Mushrooms and Mascarpone

*Adapted from Jonathan Waxman*

**Serves 6** | **Active time: 50 minutes** | **Start to finish: 50 minutes**

White polenta is a specialty of the Veneto, but many Americans will recognize it as hominy grits, which make a wonderful substitute. Although it's usually served with fish, white polenta makes a delicious bed for sautéed wild mushrooms and dollops of mascarpone.

**FOR POLENTA**

- 4½ cups water
- 1 cup coarse stone-ground white grits
- ¼ cup heavy cream
- 2 tablespoons grated Parmigiano-Reggiano
- 1½ teaspoon salt
- ½ teaspoon black pepper

**FOR MUSHROOMS**

- 1 pound assorted fresh wild mushrooms, such as porcini, oyster, chanterelle, lobster, and hedgehog
- 3 tablespoons extra-virgin olive oil
- 1 garlic clove, smashed
- ¼ cup water
- 3 tablespoons cold unsalted butter
- 1½ tablespoons fresh lemon juice
- 1 tablespoon chopped fresh flat-leaf parsley

**FOR SERVING**

- ½ cup mascarpone
- 2 tablespoons grated Parmigiano-Reggiano

▶ **MAKE POLENTA:** Bring water to a simmer in a 3- to 4-quart heavy saucepan. Add grits in a slow stream, whisking until incorporated. Simmer, stirring occasionally with a long-handled whisk or wooden spoon, until liquid is absorbed and polenta is thick and soft, about 30 minutes. (Grits will have a loose, risotto-like consistency.) Remove from heat and stir in cream, cheese, 1 teaspoon salt, and ¼ teaspoon pepper. Keep warm, covered.

▶ **SAUTÉ MUSHROOMS WHILE POLENTA SIMMERS:** If using porcini, halve if large, then slice lengthwise into ¼-inch-thick slices. If using oysters, trim spongy base if necessary and slice caps into ½-inch-wide strips. If using chanterelles, leave small mushrooms whole, halve if medium, and quarter if large. If using lobsters, cut into ½-inch pieces. If using hedgehogs, trim base of stems and halve caps if large.

▶ Heat oil in a 10-inch heavy skillet over medium-high heat until it shimmers, then sauté mushrooms and garlic with remaining ½ teaspoon salt and remaining ¼ teaspoon pepper, until mushrooms are golden and any liquid they give off is evaporated, 6 to 8 minutes.

▶ Add water, butter, lemon juice, and parsley and heat, swirling skillet, until butter melts and liquid forms a sauce.

▶ **TO SERVE:** Top each serving of polenta with mushrooms, mascarpone, and Parmigiano-Reggiano. Serve immediately (polenta stiffens as it cools).

**COOKS' NOTES:** The mushroom sauce can be made 1 hour ahead and kept, covered, at room temperature. Reheat before using.

Coarse stone-ground white grits are available by mail order from hoppinjohns.com.

# Mushroom Risotto

**Serves 4 to 6** | **Active time: 45 minutes** | **Start to finish: 1 hour**

Adding a little soy sauce to the mushroom broth might not be Italian, but it deepens the flavor, taking this risotto in an even woodsier direction. Leftovers are terrific in Mushroom and Mozzarella Arancini, page 30.

**KITCHEN TIP**

## STIR IT UP—OR NOT

Although plenty of risotto recipes have you stirring constantly the whole time, we've found that as long as we're diligent during the first 5 to 10 minutes, we can relax a bit after that and turn away from the pot occasionally to wash a dish or grate some cheese.

1   ounce (28 grams) dried porcini (1 cup)
3¾  cups hot water
5¼  cups reduced-sodium chicken broth (42 ounces)
1   tablespoon soy sauce
1   tablespoon olive oil
6   tablespoons (¾ stick) unsalted butter
1   medium onion, finely chopped
2   garlic cloves, finely chopped
¾   pound cremini mushrooms, trimmed and thinly sliced
1   pound Arborio rice (2⅓ cups)
⅔   cup dry white wine
½   cup grated Parmigiano-Reggiano
1   teaspoon salt
½   teaspoon black pepper
¼   cup chopped fresh flat-leaf parsley

**SPECIAL EQUIPMENT**

Parchment paper (if reserving some risotto for another recipe)

**GARNISH**

Parmigiano-Reggiano shavings

▶ Soak porcini in 1½ cups hot water in a bowl until softened, about 20 minutes. Lift porcini out, squeezing liquid back into bowl. Rinse to remove any grit and coarsely chop. Pour soaking liquid through a sieve lined with a coffee filter or a dampened paper towel into a 3- to 4-quart saucepan, then add broth, soy sauce, and remaining 2¼ cups water to pan and bring to a simmer.

▶ Meanwhile, heat oil with 1 tablespoon butter in a 4- to 5-quart heavy pot over medium-high heat until foam subsides, then sauté onion until softened, about 5 minutes. Add garlic and fresh mushrooms and sauté until mushrooms are browned and any liquid they give off is evaporated, about 8 minutes. Stir in porcini and sauté for 1 minute, then add rice and cook, stirring, 1 minute. Add wine and cook, stirring, until absorbed, about 1 minute.

▶ Stir 1 cup simmering broth into rice and cook, stirring constantly and keeping at a strong simmer, until absorbed. Continue cooking and adding broth, about 1 cup at a time, stirring frequently and letting each addition be absorbed before adding next, until rice is tender and creamy looking but still al dente, 18 to 20 minutes. Remove from heat. Stir in cheese, salt, pepper, and remaining 5 tablespoons butter until butter is melted. Thin risotto, if necessary, with some of remaining broth (you will have some broth left over).

▶ If reserving some risotto to make the *arancini* on page 30, set aside 3 cups and cool to room temperature, then chill. (Remaining risotto serves 4 as a main course.)

▶ Stir parsley into remaining risotto. Garnish with cheese and serve immediately.

**COOKS' NOTE:** The leftover risotto keeps, covered and chilled, 4 days.

< *Osso Buco with Tomatoes, Olives, and Gremolata, page 102*

# CHAPTER 4

# SEAFOOD, CHICKEN & MEAT

One of the hallmarks of Italian cooking is simplicity: If you start with the best ingredients and prepare them with a minimum of fuss, the pure flavors will shine through. Years of poverty taught Italian cooks to treat precious meat, chicken, and seafood with special reverence and to coax maximum flavor from their limited supply. There's a waste-not reason for everything: The juices from a roast poussin flavor the farro cooked inside it; a tough veal shank is transformed into succulent osso buco through slow-braising; leftovers become savory *ragùs* or pasta fillings. Seafood is likewise very simply prepared: a quick simmer in tomato broth for mussels or clams, a flash in the pan for the calamari used in a sprightly salad—a marriage of frugality and abundance that is nothing short of miraculous.

# Calamari Salad

Serves **4** | Active time: **30 minutes** | Start to finish: **45 minutes**

In this incredibly easy salad, a lemony vinaigrette plays a dual role: mellowing the raw onion while sparking the dish's flavor.

1½  pounds cleaned squid
2  tablespoons fresh lemon juice
1  tablespoon red-wine vinegar
⅓  cup extra-virgin olive oil
1  large garlic clove, minced
   Salt and black pepper
1  small red onion, halved lengthwise, then thinly sliced crosswise (1 cup)
⅓  cup pitted Kalamata olives, halved lengthwise
2  cups cherry or grape tomatoes (¾ pound), halved or quartered if large
2  celery ribs, cut into ¼-inch-thick slices
1  cup fresh flat-leaf parsley leaves

▶ Rinse squid under cold running water, then lightly pat dry between paper towels. Halve tentacles lengthwise and cut bodies (including flaps, if attached) crosswise into ⅓-inch-wide rings.

▶ Have ready a bowl of ice and cold water. Cook squid in a 5- to 6-quart pot of well-salted boiling water, uncovered, until just opaque, 40 to 60 seconds. Drain in a colander and immediately transfer to ice bath to stop cooking. When squid is cool, drain and pat dry.

▶ Whisk together lemon juice, vinegar, oil, garlic, ½ teaspoon salt, and ¼ teaspoon black pepper in a large bowl, then stir in onion and let stand for 5 minutes.

▶ Add squid, olives, tomatoes, celery, and parsley to dressing and toss well. Season with salt and pepper, then let stand for at least 15 minutes to allow flavors to develop.

**COOKS' NOTE:** Although delicious when eaten right away, this salad tastes even better if you chill it, covered, for 8 hours, and then bring it to room temperature (about 1 hour), stirring occasionally.

# Mussels with Tomato Broth

**Serves 4** | Active time: **25 minutes** | Start to finish: **25 minutes**

These are a snap to prepare and make a hearty meal when paired with a loaf of crusty bread to mop up the rich tomato broth.

- 3 garlic cloves, finely chopped
- ¼ teaspoon hot red-pepper flakes (optional)
- 3 tablespoons extra-virgin olive oil
- 1 cup dry white wine
- 1 cup Basic Tomato Sauce (page 164)
- 4 pounds cultivated mussels, scrubbed and beards removed

▶ Cook garlic and red-pepper flakes (if using) in oil in a 6- to 8-quart heavy pot over medium-low heat, stirring, until garlic is pale golden, 1 to 2 minutes. Add wine and boil over high heat for 2 minutes.

▶ Add tomato sauce and mussels and cook over medium-high heat, covered, stirring occasionally, until mussels just open wide, 6 to 8 minutes. (Discard any mussels that are unopened after 8 minutes.) Serve immediately.

KITCHEN TIP

## THE CULTIVATED MUSSEL

Cultivated mussels are one of the great win-win stories in farmed seafood. They're raised in an environmentally responsible way, resulting in much cleaner shells, with fewer beards to scrape off, which cuts way down on the prep time in the kitchen. When buying them, ask to see the harvest date and steer clear of any that are more than four days old. But don't ignore the classic test: Take a good whiff and make sure you detect that delightful briny smell and not the remnants of low tide. Rinse the mussels quickly after purchasing them, and toss out any with cracked shells. Keep them covered with a wet towel in a bowl in the fridge, and plan on cooking them the same day. Just before they go into the pot, tap any opened mussels on the counter; if they don't close their shells, give them the heave-ho.

# Grilled Halibut with Fava Bean and Roasted Tomato Sauce

*Adapted from Jonathan Waxman*

**Serves 6** | **Active time: 1½ hours** | **Start to finish: 1¾ hours**

Since fava and lima beans have a shorter growing season than most local tomatoes, we've given frozen edamame, available year-round, as an alternative to make this recipe more versatile.

- 4 **large tomatoes (preferably heirloom; 2 pounds total)**
- 3 **garlic cloves, cut lengthwise into slivers**
- **Salt and black pepper**
- 2 **tablespoons olive oil**
- 2 **pounds fresh fava or lima beans in pod, shelled, or 10 ounces frozen baby lima beans or shelled edamame (soybeans; 2 cups), not thawed**
- ½ **cup chopped fresh basil**
- 1–2 **tablespoons fresh lemon juice**
- 6 **(6-ounce) pieces halibut fillet (1¼–1½ inches thick)**

▶ Preheat oven to 450°F, with rack in middle.

▶ Core tomatoes, then halve crosswise. Stud the cut side of each half with garlic slivers, then sprinkle with ½ teaspoon salt and ¼ teaspoon pepper (total). Arrange tomatoes, cut sides up, on a lightly oiled baking sheet, then drizzle evenly with 1 tablespoon oil. Roast until just soft and wilted, 15 to 20 minutes.

▶ While tomatoes roast, cook beans in a 6- to 8-quart pot of salted boiling water, uncovered, until just tender, 5 to 8 minutes. Drain in a colander and cool slightly, about 10 minutes. When beans are cool enough to handle, gently slip off skins. (Don't bother peeling edamame.)

Coarsely chop beans and roasted tomatoes, then toss with basil, remaining tablespoon oil, ½ teaspoon salt, ¼ teaspoon pepper, and lemon juice (to taste).

▶ Prepare grill for cooking over medium-hot charcoal (medium heat for gas); see page 11.

▶ Pat fish dry and season both sides with salt and pepper. Grill on lightly oiled grill rack, covered only if using gas grill, turning over once, until just cooked through, 6 to 8 minutes total.

▶ Serve fish topped with bean and roasted tomato sauce.

**COOKS' NOTES:** If you aren't able to grill outdoors, the fish can be cooked in a hot lightly oiled large (two-burner) ridged grill pan over medium-high heat.

The beans can be cooked and peeled 1 day ahead, then chilled in a sealed plastic bag.

The bean and roasted tomato sauce can be made 1 day ahead and chilled, covered. Bring to room temperature before serving.

# Sea Bass with Tomatoes and Capers

Serves **4** | Active time: **15 minutes** | Start to finish: **30 minutes**

Like the French, the Italians know that fish enclosed in a no-mess pouch of paper or foil steams to perfection in its own juices. Here, sea bass is infused with the sunny taste of tomatoes, capers, garlic, and lemon.

- 3 tablespoons extra-virgin olive oil
- 4 (6-ounce) fillets black sea bass or striped bass (½- to 1¼-inches thick) with skin
- Salt
- ¼ teaspoon black pepper
- 8 thin lemon slices (less than ⅛-inch thick; from 1 large lemon)
- 8 sprigs thyme
- 2 garlic cloves, very thinly sliced
- 12 cherry or grape tomatoes, halved
- 1½ tablespoons drained bottled capers

▸ Preheat oven to 400°F, with rack in middle. Line a large baking sheet with foil, then drizzle with 1 tablespoon oil.

▸ Pat fish dry and sprinkle both sides with a total of ¾ teaspoon salt and ¼ teaspoon pepper. Arrange fillets, skin sides down, in one layer in center of foil on baking sheet and slide 2 lemon slices under each fillet. Put 2 thyme sprigs on top of each fillet.

▸ Heat remaining 2 tablespoons oil in a 10-inch heavy skillet over medium-high heat until it shimmers, then sauté garlic until pale golden, about 30 seconds. Add tomatoes and a pinch of salt and sauté until tomatoes are softened, about 1 minute. Stir in capers.

▸ Spoon hot tomato mixture over fish, then cover with another sheet of foil, tenting it slightly, and crimp edges together to seal.

▸ Bake until fish is just cooked through, 12 to 15 minutes; check by removing from oven and lifting up a corner of top sheet of foil, then pulling up sides of bottom sheet to keep liquid from leaking. (If fish is not cooked through, reseal foil and continue to bake, checking every 3 minutes.)

▸ Transfer fillets with lemon slices to plates using a spatula (be careful not to tear foil underneath) and spoon tomatoes and juices over top. Serve immediately, discarding thyme before eating.

# Seafood Stew

*Adapted from Faith Willinger*

Serves **6** | Active time: **35 minutes** | Start to finish: **35 minutes**

This simple one-pot dish is rich with the essence of the sea. Don't get too caught up in the measurements for the fish: You can vary the seafood amounts depending on what you have on hand. Serve this over polenta or paired with crusty bread to soak up the briny sauce.

- ½ cup Basic Tomato Sauce (page 164)
- 3 tablespoons dry white wine
- 3 tablespoons red-wine vinegar
- 3 garlic cloves, peeled and lightly smashed
- ½ teaspoon hot red-pepper flakes or 2 whole small dried red chiles
- 3 tablespoons extra-virgin olive oil
- 1 pound Manila clams or cockles, scrubbed well
- 1 pound cultivated mussels, scrubbed well and beards removed
- ½ pound large shrimp in shell, peeled and deveined
- ½ pound sea scallops, tough ligament removed from side of each if attached
- ½ pound (1-inch-thick) fish fillet, cut into 1-inch chunks

**GARNISH**
Chopped fresh flat-leaf parsley

**ACCOMPANIMENT**
White country loaf

▶ Stir together tomato sauce, wine, and vinegar in a small bowl.

▶ Sauté garlic and red-pepper flakes in oil in a 12-inch heavy skillet over medium-high heat, turning garlic occasionally, until garlic is pale golden, 1 to 2 minutes.

▶ Add clams and mussels and toss briefly. Arrange rest of seafood on top (don't stir), then pour tomato sauce mixture over all and cook, covered, until clams and mussels just open wide (check often after 4 minutes; discard any remaining unopened after 8) and rest of seafood is just cooked through.

▶ Transfer seafood with a slotted spoon to a serving dish, then boil sauce until thickened slightly and pour over seafood. Garnish with parsley and serve with bread.

# Chicken Marsala

Serves 4 | Active time: **50 minutes** | Start to finish: **50 minutes**

Skinless boneless chicken breasts, pounded thin, substitute beautifully for veal in this Italian restaurant favorite. Marsala, a Sicilian fortified wine, comes sweet or dry, but we prefer the hint of smoke in the dry.

1¾ cups reduced-sodium chicken broth (14 ounces)
2 tablespoons finely chopped shallot
5 tablespoons unsalted butter
10 ounces mushrooms, trimmed and thinly sliced
1½ teaspoons finely chopped fresh sage
Salt and black pepper
1 cup all-purpose flour
4 skinless boneless chicken breast halves (2 pounds total)
2 tablespoons extra-virgin olive oil
½ cup plus 2 tablespoons dry Marsala wine
⅔ cup heavy cream
1 teaspoon fresh lemon juice

▶ Preheat oven to 200°F, with rack in middle.

▶ Bring broth to a boil in a 2-quart saucepan over high heat, then boil, uncovered, until reduced to about ¾ cup, about 20 minutes.

▶ Cook shallot in 3 tablespoons butter in an 8- to 10-inch heavy skillet over medium heat, stirring, until shallot begins to turn golden, about 1 minute. Add mushrooms, 1 teaspoon sage, ¼ teaspoon salt, and ⅛ teaspoon pepper and cook, stirring occasionally, until liquid mushrooms give off is evaporated and mushrooms begin to brown, 6 to 8 minutes. Remove from heat.

▶ Put flour in a wide shallow bowl. Gently pound chicken to ¼-inch thick between 2 sheets of plastic wrap using the flat side of a meat pounder or a rolling pin.

▶ Pat chicken dry and season with salt and pepper, then dredge in flour, 1 piece at a time, shaking off excess. Transfer to sheets of wax paper, arranging chicken in 1 layer.

▶ Heat 1 tablespoon each of oil and butter in a 10-inch heavy skillet over medium-high heat until foam subsides, then sauté half of chicken, turning over once, until golden and just cooked through, about 4 minutes total. Transfer cooked chicken to a large heatproof platter, arranging in 1 layer, then put in oven to keep warm.

▶ Wipe out skillet with paper towels and cook remaining chicken in same manner, arranging in one layer in oven.

▶ Add ½ cup wine to skillet and boil over high heat, stirring and scraping up brown bits, about 30 seconds. Add reduced broth, cream, and mushrooms, then simmer, stirring occasionally, until sauce is slightly thickened, 6 to 8 minutes. Stir in lemon juice and remaining 2 tablespoons wine and remaining ½ teaspoon sage.

▶ Serve chicken with sauce.

# Quick Chicken Ragù

*Adapted from Elena Faita-Venditelli*

Serves **4** | Active time: **30 minutes** | Start to finish: **1 hour**

The word *ragù* brings to mind a slowly simmered meat sauce, but not all *ragùs* take days on the stovetop. Cutting the chicken thighs into small pieces reduces the cooking time, and pancetta adds instant depth. Result: a surprisingly hearty stew in less than an hour.

- 2 tablespoons extra-virgin olive oil
- 2 tablespoons unsalted butter
- 1 (¼-pound) piece pancetta (Italian unsmoked cured bacon), cut into ¼-inch dice (⅔ cup)
- 1 tablespoon finely chopped fresh sage
- 1½ teaspoons finely chopped fresh rosemary
- 1½ pounds skinless boneless chicken thighs, cut into 1-inch pieces
- 1 medium onion, chopped
- 1 medium carrot, chopped
- 1 celery rib, chopped
- 1 cup light dry red wine, such as Pinot Noir
- 1 (14- to 15-ounce) can diced tomatoes in juice, drained
- Coarse gray sea salt
- Coarsely ground black pepper

ACCOMPANIMENT
Our Favorite Simple Polenta (page 172)

▶ Heat oil and butter in a 12-inch heavy skillet (2 inches deep) over medium heat until hot but not smoking, then add pancetta and cook, stirring occasionally, 2 minutes. Add sage and rosemary and cook, stirring, 30 seconds. Add chicken and cook, stirring occasionally, until chicken is no longer pink on outside, 2 to 3 minutes. Add onion, carrot, and celery and cook, stirring occasionally, until softened, 5 to 7 minutes.

▶ Add wine and simmer, uncovered, stirring occasionally, until liquid is reduced to about 1 cup, about 10 minutes. Add tomatoes, ¾ teaspoon sea salt, and ½ teaspoon pepper and simmer, stirring occasionally, until sauce is thickened, 5 to 10 minutes. Season with salt and pepper and serve over polenta.

**COOKS' NOTE:** The *ragù* can be made 1 day ahead and cooled completely, uncovered, then chilled, covered.

# Roast Chicken with Pancetta and Olives

*Adapted from Tony Oltranti*

**Serves 8** | **Active time: 25 minutes** | Start to finish: 1½ hours

This simple, savory chicken is roasted with pancetta, garlic, and olives but stays moist in a shallow bath of white wine. Although it's delicious with Our Favorite Simple Polenta (page 172), you can enrich the recipe by stirring in a little butter, mascarpone, and grated Parmigiano at the end.

- 2 chickens (about 3½ pounds each), backbones cut out and each chicken cut into 12 pieces (see Kitchen Tip)
- ¼ cup extra-virgin olive oil
- 1½ tablespoons chopped fresh thyme
- 1 tablespoon chopped fresh rosemary
- 1 tablespoon fine sea salt
- ½–1 teaspoon hot red-pepper flakes
- 1 teaspoon black pepper
- 10 garlic cloves, peeled
- 2 (¼-inch-thick) slices pancetta, cut into 1-inch pieces
- 1 cup dry white wine
- 24 oil-cured black olives

▶ Preheat oven to 450°F, with rack in middle.

▶ Toss chicken with oil, thyme, rosemary, sea salt, red-pepper flakes, and black pepper, rubbing mixture into chicken.

▶ Arrange chicken, skin side up, in 1 layer in an 18-by-13-inch heavy baking sheet. Scatter garlic and pancetta on top and roast until chicken begins to brown, about 20 minutes. Drizzle wine over chicken and roast 8 minutes more. Scatter olives over chicken and roast until skin is golden brown and chicken is cooked through, 15 to 20 minutes more. Let stand for 10 minutes.

**COOKS' NOTE:** To cut a chicken into 12 pieces, remove wings, then separate drumsticks and thighs. Halve breast, then cut each half into 3 pieces. The backbones can be used to make chicken stock.

**KITCHEN TIP**
## CHICKEN PARTS

If the first ingredient in this recipe—a chicken cut into 12 pieces—confounds you, don't let that stop you from making this truly delicious dish. You can ask your butcher to cut up the chicken or simply buy your chicken in parts instead of starting with the whole bird. This recipe works just as well with 6 pounds of thighs, or just breasts. If you chose to include breasts (get the ones with skin and bone), be ready with a sharp heavy knife to cut each breast half crosswise through the bones into 3 relatively equal pieces.

# Roasted Poussins with Farro Stuffing

**Serves 4** | **Active time: 50 minutes** | **Start to finish: 2 hours**

Farro, also known as emmer wheat, was the staple grain of the Roman Empire. Its delightful chewiness, similar to barley's, makes it a wonderful base for a stuffing studded with currants, olives, and pine nuts.

**FOR FARRO STUFFING**

- 1¼ cups farro
- 1½ cups finely chopped onion (1 large)
- 2 tablespoons olive oil
- ⅓ cup dried currants
- ⅛ teaspoon ground cinnamon
- ½ teaspoon salt
- ¼ teaspoon black pepper
- ⅓ cup chopped pitted Kalamata olives
- ⅓ cup pine nuts, toasted

**FOR POUSSINS**

- 4 poussins (about 1 pound each)
- 2 teaspoons salt
- ¼ teaspoon black pepper
- 3 tablespoons unsalted butter, melted and cooled

**FOR JUS**

- ⅓ cup reduced-sodium chicken broth
- ⅓ cup water
- ½ teaspoon cornstarch, whisked together with 2 teaspoons water
- ½ teaspoon fresh lemon juice
- Salt and black pepper

**SPECIAL EQUIPMENT**

Kitchen string; large flameproof roasting pan fitted with a large flat rack; instant-read thermometer

▶ **MAKE FARRO STUFFING:** Soak farro in a bowl of cold water, changing water twice, for 25 minutes total. Drain in a sieve.

▶ Cook farro, uncovered, in a 3- to 4-quart pot of salted boiling water, stirring occasionally, until just tender, about 25 minutes; drain well and transfer to a bowl.

▶ While farro is boiling, cook onion in oil in a 12-inch heavy skillet over medium heat, stirring frequently, until softened, about 7 minutes. Add currants and cook, stirring, until they plump, 2 to 3 minutes. Add cinnamon, salt, and pepper, and cook, stirring, 1 minute; stir into drained farro with olives and pine nuts. Cool completely, about 20 minutes.

▶ **STUFF AND ROAST POUSSINS:** Preheat oven to 450°F, with racks in upper and lower thirds. Rinse poussins all over; pat dry. Cut out necks (if attached) with poultry shears and discard. Sprinkle salt and pepper inside and outside of birds; stuff each with ½ cup stuffing. Put remaining stuffing in a small baking dish and cover with foil. Tie legs together with string and arrange poussins, without crowding, on rack in pan, then brush with some of melted butter.

▶ Roast poussins in upper third of oven, basting once or twice with remaining butter, until deep golden, 30 to 35 minutes. Reduce oven to 375°F and add stuffing to lower third of oven. Roast poussins until a thermometer inserted into a thigh (avoiding bone) registers 180°F, and into stuffing inside bird, 165°F, 10 to 20 minutes more. Transfer poussins to a platter, reserving pan, and loosely cover with foil. Continue cooking stuffing while making *jus*.

▶ **MAKE JUS:** Remove rack from pan and tilt pan so fat and juices accumulate in one corner. Carefully spoon off almost all of fat. Straddle pan across two burners; add broth and water and deglaze pan by boiling over high heat, stirring and scraping up brown bits, 1 minute. Transfer to a small saucepan and simmer until reduced to about ½ cup, 3 minutes. Stir cornstarch mixture; stir into sauce and simmer, whisking, 1 minute. Add lemon juice; season with salt and pepper, then pour through a fine-mesh sieve into a gravy boat.

▶ Cut off string and serve poussins with *jus* and additional stuffing.

# Straccetti di Manzo

Sliced Steak with Arugula

**Serves 4** | Active time: **10 minutes** | Start to finish: **10 minutes**

Generations of Roman cooks have relied on this trattoria favorite—sautéed steak over arugula with a warm vinaigrette made with classic ingredients— for dinner in a hurry.

5  ounces baby arugula
⅓  cup extra-virgin olive oil
2  large garlic cloves, smashed
1  large sprig rosemary
1  pound boneless top loin steak (New York strip) or sirloin (1 inch thick), cut crosswise into ⅛-inch-thick slices
1  teaspoon salt
   Black pepper
1  large shallot, thinly sliced crosswise
1½  tablespoons balsamic vinegar
1½  tablespoons red-wine vinegar

▶ Mound arugula on a large platter.
▶ Heat oil with garlic and rosemary in a 12-inch heavy skillet over high heat, turning garlic once or twice, until garlic is golden, about 4 minutes. Discard garlic and rosemary.
▶ Meanwhile, toss steak slices with ¾ teaspoon salt and ½ teaspoon pepper. Add meat to skillet all at once and sauté over high heat, tossing with tongs to color evenly, about 1 minute for medium-rare. Arrange steak over arugula using tongs, then add shallot to oil in skillet along with vinegars, remaining ¼ teaspoon salt, and ¼ teaspoon pepper and boil for 2 minutes. Pour dressing over steak, grind additional pepper over, and serve immediately.

# Short Ribs Braised in Red Wine

Serves **6** | Active time: **35 minutes** | Start to finish: **3½ hours**

The Piemontese classic, beef braised in Barolo, becomes positively spectacular when made with short ribs, which dissolve into mouthwatering chunks of meat in a complex sauce.

**KITCHEN TIP**

## THE SKINNY ON SHORT RIBS

Ask any chef: Short ribs are one of the most popular items on menus, and it's easy to see why. This well-marbled cut from the rib bones in the chuck (or shoulder) portion of the steer is meant for the slow, moist heat of braising, which makes the meat fall-off-the-bone tender. And because the bone is attached, the flavor is that much deeper and beefier. When shopping for short ribs, you'll either find them cut lengthwise into individual bones (they're wide and rather flat) or cut across the bones into strips—often labeled flanken—that each contain 3 to 4 short pieces of bone. Either cut produces a memorable result, but the 4-inch-long individual ribs called for in this recipe are the most dramatic to serve.

1 (750 ml) bottle Barolo or other full-bodied dry red wine (see Cooks' Note)
4–4¼ pounds beef short ribs, cut into individual 4-inch-long ribs
2 teaspoons salt
1 teaspoon black pepper
3 tablespoons olive oil
2 ounces sliced pancetta, chopped
1 medium onion, chopped
5 large garlic cloves, finely chopped
3 medium carrots, chopped
3 celery ribs, chopped
4 (4- to 6-inch) thyme sprigs
2 (6- to 8-inch) rosemary sprigs
1 (14- to 15-ounce) can diced tomatoes in juice
2 cups water

**SPECIAL EQUIPMENT**
12-inch-wide heavy nonreactive ovenproof pot (at least 3½ inches deep) with a tight lid

**ACCOMPANIMENT**
Buttered egg pasta tossed with cho pped fresh parsley

▶ Preheat oven to 325°F, with rack in lower third.
▶ Boil wine in a 2- to 3-quart pot until reduced to 1 cup, 20 to 25 minutes.
▶ Meanwhile, pat ribs dry; rub with salt and pepper.
▶ Heat oil in pot over high heat until it shimmers and quickly brown ribs on all 3 meaty sides (but not bone side) without crowding, in batches, about 1 minute per side. Transfer meat to a large plate. Pour off all but 1 tablespoon fat and cook pancetta over medium heat, stirring, until browned and fat is rendered. Add onion and cook, stirring occasionally, until softened and lightly browned, about 6 minutes. Add garlic and cook, stirring, until pale golden, about 2 minutes. Add carrots, celery, and herbs and cook, stirring occasionally, 2 minutes.
▶ Stir in tomatoes with their juice and return ribs with any juices to pot, arranging them bone side down.
▶ Add reduced wine and water and bring liquid to a boil, uncovered. Cover pot and transfer to oven, then braise until meat is very tender, 2 to 2½ hours.
▶ Skim off excess fat from surface of sauce and discard herb stems. If a thicker sauce is desired, transfer ribs carefully to a plate (meat will fall off bones easily) and boil sauce, stirring occasionally, to thicken slightly. Return short ribs to sauce. Serve with buttered pasta and parsley.

**COOKS' NOTES:** Barolo is pricey, so feel free to save it for drinking and use a cheaper wine like Nebbiolo or Malbec.

Short ribs improve in flavor if braised 1 day ahead and cooled, uncovered, then chilled, covered. Bring back to a simmer on top of the stove, then reheat, covered, in a 350°F oven until hot, about 30 minutes.

# Osso Buco with Tomatoes, Olives, and Gremolata

**Serves 8** | Active time: **45 minutes** | Start to finish: **3¾ hours**

The richness of braised veal shanks is cut by the salty edge of olives, the gentle acidity of tomato, and the fresh lemon note of the *gremolata*. Serve over Our Favorite Simple Polenta (page 172).

**FOR STEW**

- 8 (10- to 12-ounce) meaty cross-cut veal shanks (osso buco; 5–6½ pounds total), each tied with kitchen string
- Salt and black pepper
- ½ cup all-purpose flour
- 3 tablespoons olive oil
- 3 tablespoons unsalted butter
- 2 medium onions, halved lengthwise and thinly sliced
- 1 small carrot, finely chopped
- 1 celery rib, finely chopped
- 2 garlic cloves, finely chopped
- 1 (28-ounce) can whole plum tomatoes with juice, drained, reserving juice, and coarsely chopped
- 1 cup dry white wine
- 1 cup reduced-sodium chicken broth
- 1 cup Gaeta or Kalamata olives, pitted and halved
- 1½ teaspoons fresh thyme leaves
- 2 flat-leaf parsley sprigs
- 1 Turkish or ½ California bay leaf
- 2 (2-by-½-inch) strips lemon zest, cut crosswise into fine julienne

**FOR GREMOLATA**

- 3 tablespoons chopped fresh flat-leaf parsley
- 1 large garlic clove, minced
- 1 teaspoon finely grated lemon zest

**ACCOMPANIMENT**

Our Favorite Simple Polenta (page 172)

**SPECIAL EQUIPMENT**

7- to 9-quart heavy ovenproof pot (wide enough to hold shanks in one layer; see Cooks' Notes)

▶ **MAKE STEW:** Preheat oven to 325°F, with rack in middle.

▶ Pat shanks dry and season with salt and pepper. Divide shanks and flour between two large sealable plastic bags and shake to coat, then remove shanks from bags, shaking off excess flour. Heat oil and 2 tablespoons butter in ovenproof pot over medium-high heat until foam subsides, then brown shanks well in 2 batches, 10 to 12 minutes per batch, transferring to a plate.

▶ Reduce heat to medium and add remaining tablespoon butter to pot along with onions, carrot, celery, and garlic and cook, stirring, until onions are pale golden, about 5 minutes. Add tomatoes with their juice and remaining stew ingredients along with 1 teaspoon salt and ½ teaspoon black pepper and bring to a boil, stirring.

▶ Arrange shanks in pot in one layer and return to a simmer. Cover pot and braise shanks in middle of oven until very tender, about 2½ hours. Remove strings from osso buco and discard along with parsley sprigs and bay leaf.

▶ **MAKE GREMOLATA AND SERVE OSSO BUCO:** Stir together *gremolata* ingredients in a small bowl, sprinkle over osso buco and serve with polenta.

**COOKS' NOTES:** The osso buco (without the *gremolata*) can be made 1 day ahead. Cool, uncovered, then chill, covered. Reheat, covered, in a 325°F oven for 30 to 40 minutes.

The osso buco can also be cooked in a large heavy nonreactive roasting pan. Straddle pan across two burners for browning and boiling, then cover pan tightly with heavy-duty foil for braising.

# Veal Scallopini with Capers

Serves **4** | Active time: **10 minutes** | Start to finish: **10 minutes**

Quick-cooking scallopini are perfect for breathing new life into busy weeknights. And the brown butter doesn't hurt either.

½  cup all-purpose flour
1¼  teaspoons salt
¾  teaspoon black pepper
1  pound thin veal scallopini (less than ¼-inch thick)
3  tablespoons olive or vegetable oil
4  tablespoons (½ stick) unsalted butter, cut into pieces
1½  tablespoons red-wine vinegar
1½  tablespoons drained small capers
2  tablespoons chopped fresh flat-leaf parsley

▸ Stir together flour, 1 teaspoon salt, and ½ teaspoon pepper, then pat veal dry and dredge in flour, knocking off excess. Arrange, as coated, in one layer on a sheet of wax paper.
▸ Meanwhile, heat a 12-inch heavy skillet (not nonstick) over high heat until hot, then add oil and heat until it shimmers.
▸ Cook veal in 2 batches, turning once, until browned and cooked through, 2 to 2½ minutes per batch. Transfer to a plate.
▸ Discard oil from skillet, then add butter and cook over medium heat, shaking skillet frequently, until browned and fragrant, 1 to 2 minutes. Stir in vinegar, capers, and remaining ¼ teaspoon each of salt and pepper. Return veal to skillet just to heat through, then sprinkle with parsley, and serve.

**COOKS' NOTE:** The scallopini can be made with thinly sliced chicken breast.

# Pork Chops Saltimbocca with Sautéed Spinach

Serves **2** | Active time: **15 minutes** | Start to finish: **20 minutes**

Any excuse to cook a pork chop is a good excuse, and here is one of Italian origin: You get to stuff it with prosciutto, not to mention buttery Fontina and aromatic sage.

2  (1-inch-thick) center-cut rib pork chops
2  fresh sage leaves, finely chopped
2  very thin slices Italian Fontina
2  thin slices prosciutto
   Salt
¼  teaspoon black pepper
2  tablespoons olive oil
1  large garlic clove, finely chopped
1  (10-ounce) bag fresh spinach, stems discarded
2  tablespoons unsalted butter, cut into pieces
1  tablespoon fresh lemon juice

▶ Preheat oven to 450°F, with rack in middle.

▶ Cut a deep, wide pocket in each pork chop. Sprinkle half of sage into each pocket and stuff pockets with cheese and prosciutto. Pat chops dry and season with ¼ teaspoon each salt and pepper.

▶ Heat 1 tablespoon oil in a 12-inch ovenproof heavy skillet over medium-high heat until it shimmers. Cook chops until undersides are golden, about 2 minutes, then turn chops and transfer skillet to oven. Roast until cooked through, about 5 minutes.

▶ While chops cook, heat remaining tablespoon oil in a 5-quart pot over medium heat until it shimmers. Sauté garlic until pale golden, about 30 seconds. Add spinach and cook, covered, stirring occasionally, until wilted, about 3 minutes. Season with salt.

▶ Transfer chops to a platter. Add butter and lemon juice to hot skillet, stirring and scraping up brown bits, then pour sauce over pork. Serve pork with spinach.

**COOKS' NOTE:** The recipe can be doubled.

# Lamb Chops Scottadito

*Adapted from Rose Gray and Ruth Rogers*

Serves **6** | Active time: **45 minutes** | Start to finish: **55 minutes**

*Scottadito* means "scorches the finger" and refers to a plain grilled lamb chop, usually pounded before cooking, that is meant to be held like a lollipop.

3 frenched racks of lamb (each rack about 1½ pounds with 8 ribs), trimmed of all but a thin layer of fat and cut into chops by butcher (or 24 rib lamb chops, trimmed well)

⅔ cup lard

3 tablespoons extra-virgin olive oil

Maldon sea salt

Coarsely ground black pepper

1 lemon, halved

**SPECIAL EQUIPMENT**

Parchment paper

▶ Preheat oven to 200°F and put a heatproof platter in oven.

▶ Gently pound each chop between two sheets of parchment paper using flat side of a meat pounder, flat side of a cleaver, or a rolling pin until ¼-inch thick and doubled in diameter.

▶ Melt lard with oil in a small saucepan over low heat until translucent but not hot. Remove from heat and dip each chop in lard, transferring to a parchment-lined baking sheet and arranging in one layer. Chill until lard is solidified, about 10 minutes.

▶ Heat a 12-inch heavy skillet (not nonstick) over medium-high heat until hot. Season chops with sea salt and pepper to taste, then brown in batches of 4 (without crowding), turning over once, about 4 minutes total per batch for medium-rare. Transfer cooked chops to heated platter.

▶ Squeeze lemon halves over hot chops and serve immediately.

# Anchovy and Rosemary Roasted Lamb

Serves 6 | Active time: **30 minutes** | Start to finish: **3½ hours**

Lamb with anchovy herb paste is a classic Italian preparation. The anchovy doesn't come across as fishy tasting—it simply lends a savory note that blends beautifully with the meat.

**FOR LAMB**

- 6   garlic cloves
- 9   flat anchovy fillets, drained and patted dry
- ¼   cup olive oil
- 2½  tablespoons chopped fresh rosemary
- 1   (6- to 7-pound) semiboneless leg of lamb (aitchbone removed), all but a thin layer of fat discarded and lamb tied
-     Salt and black pepper

**FOR SALSA VERDE**

- ½   cup extra-virgin olive oil
- 9   flat anchovy fillets, drained, patted dry, and minced
- 2½  tablespoons drained bottled capers (preferably nonpareil), rinsed and finely chopped
- 6   tablespoons finely chopped fresh flat-leaf parsley
- 3   tablespoons finely chopped fresh mint
- 1   teaspoon white-wine vinegar
- ⅛   teaspoon black pepper

**SPECIAL EQUIPMENT**

   17-by-11-inch roasting pan (or larger) with a rack

▶ Mince garlic and anchovies and mash to a paste with a large heavy knife, then stir together with oil and rosemary in a small bowl. Pat lamb dry and place, fat side up, on rack in pan. Make several small 1-inch-deep slits in lamb with a paring knife, then rub marinade over entire surface, pushing some into slits. Marinate loosely covered, at room temperature for 1 hour.

▶ Preheat oven to 400°F, with rack in middle.

▶ Sprinkle lamb all over with 2 teaspoons salt and ¾ teaspoon black pepper, then roast until thermometer inserted into thickest part of lamb (almost to bone but not touching it) registers 125°F for medium-rare, 1½ to 1 ¾ hours (temperatures in thinner parts of leg may register up to 160°F). Let stand for 30 minutes before slicing.

▶ **MAKE SALSA VERDE:** Stir together all ingredients in a bowl.

▶ To carve, grab leg by shank end. Lift leg up to a level where it's comfortable for your other arm (your wrist) to carve on a downward slope. Tilting knife blade at roughly a 20-degree angle to meat, begin paring thin slices from opposite end of leg, just to one side of it, starting each slice above the previous one so that slices lengthen and widen as you move up leg.

▶ Then rotate leg a quarter turn and continue to carve, lifting each slice off with knife and draping it over the previous slice.

▶ Keep turning and slicing until you reach bone. You will end up with a range of medium-rare to well-done meat. Serve with salsa verde.

**COOKS' NOTES:** The lamb can be marinated, covered and chilled, for up to 5 hours. Bring to room temperature, about 1 hour, before roasting.

The salsa verde can be made 1 day ahead and chilled, covered.

# CHAPTER 5

# VEGETABLES

"With vegetables" could be added to the title of each preceding chapter, for they turn up throughout an Italian meal. They make excellent antipasti and pizza toppings, fill pasta sauces, and provide the perfect foil to savory meats. But Italian side dishes are where the country's reverence for its ingredients is on full display. Simple preparations—carrots braised with shallots and sage, peas tossed with asparagus and basil—allow the components to shine. So central are vegetables to the Italian table that it's startling to realize how many of them hail from the New World. Tomatoes, peppers, zucchini, butternut squash, even the corn in polenta and the potatoes for gnocchi—none existed in Italy before the sixteenth century. But one taste of these White Beans with Roasted Tomatoes makes it clear that Italian cooks have more than made up for lost time.

# Chiffonade of Romaine and Bibb Lettuces

Serves **6** | Active time: **20 minutes** | Start to finish: **20 minutes**

If you've never had thinly sliced salad greens, you're in for a treat. Your guests will be grateful because a chiffonade—from the French word *chiffon,* meaning rag—is so much easier to eat gracefully than big leaves of lettuce.

1½ tablespoons fresh lemon juice
¼ teaspoon Dijon mustard
 Salt and black pepper
⅓ cup extra-virgin olive oil
2 hearts romaine, trimmed, quartered lengthwise, then cut crosswise into ¼-inch strips
¾ pound Bibb lettuce (3 medium heads), trimmed, quartered lengthwise, then cut crosswise into ¼-inch strips

▶ Whisk together lemon juice, mustard, and salt and pepper to taste in a small bowl, then add oil in a slow stream, whisking until emulsified.
▶ Toss lettuces with just enough dressing to coat.

# Shaved Brussels Sprout Salad

*Adapted from Jonathan Waxman*

Serves **6** | Active time: **25 minutes** | Start to finish: **35 minutes**

Brussels sprouts, sliced very thin, result in an unbelievably delectable slaw. If you have a sharp knife, you could slice them by hand, but it's much easier to use an adjustable-blade slicer.

1½  pounds Brussels sprouts, any discolored leaves discarded and stems left intact
1  cup walnuts (3½ ounces), lightly toasted
2  tablespoons grated Pecorino Romano, or to taste
¼  cup olive oil
3  tablespoons fresh lemon juice
   Black pepper

**SPECIAL EQUIPMENT**
   Adjustable-blade slicer

▶ Holding each Brussels sprout by stem end, cut into very thin slices using slicer. Toss in a bowl to separate layers.
▶ Lightly crush walnuts with your hands and add to Brussels sprouts along with cheese, oil, and lemon juice, then toss to combine. Season with pepper to taste.

**COOKS' NOTES:** The walnuts can be toasted 1 day ahead and kept in an airtight container at room temperature.

The Brussels sprouts can be sliced 3 hours ahead and chilled, covered. Toss with the remaining ingredients just before serving.

Pecorino Romano varies in saltiness: You may want to add a little more than we call for here.

# Escarole and Edamame Salad

Serves **4** | Active time: **25 minutes** | Start to finish: **25 minutes**

Convenient frozen edamame take the place of harder-to-find (and highly seasonal) fava beans in this Italian-inspired salad.

- 2 **cups frozen shelled edamame (soybeans; 9 ounces)**
- 1 **tablespoon red-wine vinegar**
- ½ **teaspoon sugar**
- ¾ **teaspoon salt**
- ¼ **teaspoon black pepper**
- 3 **tablespoons extra-virgin olive oil**
- 1½ **pounds escarole, trimmed and cut crosswise into very thin strips (8 cups)**
- ⅓ **cup finely chopped fresh mint**
- ⅔ **cup grated Parmigiano-Reggiano**

▶ Cook edamame in a 3-quart pot of well-salted boiling water for 5 minutes. Drain in a sieve and rinse under cold water to stop cooking. Drain edamame again and pat dry.

▶ Whisk together vinegar, sugar, salt, and pepper in a small bowl until sugar and salt are dissolved. Add oil in a slow stream, whisking until combined.

▶ Toss together edamame, escarole, and mint in a large bowl. Add cheese and drizzle salad with dressing, then toss again. Serve immediately.

# Artichokes Braised with Garlic and Thyme

**Serves 6** | **Active time: 25 minutes** | **Start to finish: 1 hour**

A profusion of artichokes in the markets is synonymous with spring in Rome. Although the Romans have many ways to cook up this bounty—fried being one of the best—we are fond of this slow braise, which infuses the artichokes with a subtle hint of garlic.

- 1 lemon, halved
- 6 medium artichokes (½ pound each)
- 18 flat-leaf parsley sprigs
- ¼ cup olive oil
- 8 thyme sprigs
- 1 head garlic, cloves separated and left unpeeled
- 1 cup water
- 1 teaspoon salt
- ¼ teaspoon black pepper
- 1 tablespoon extra-virgin olive oil

**SPECIAL EQUIPMENT**

6- to 8-quart heavy pot wide enough to hold artichokes in a single layer (about 11 inches in diameter)

▶ Fill a large bowl with cold water and squeeze lemon halves into bowl.

▶ Working with 1 artichoke at a time, cut off top inch of artichoke and gently pull open center. Scoop out sharp leaves and fuzzy choke from center with a melon-ball cutter or a spoon. Trim bottom ¼ inch of stem (if present) to expose inner core, keeping stem attached, and trim stem down to inner core. Put artichoke in bowl of lemon water. Repeat with remaining artichokes.

▶ Remove artichokes from water and push 3 parsley sprigs into center of each. Heat ¼ cup olive oil in pot over medium heat until it shimmers, then add artichokes, thyme sprigs, garlic, ¼ cup water, ½ teaspoon salt, and black pepper. Cover pot and braise artichokes, turning occasionally, until artichokes are browned in spots and bases are tender when pierced with a knife, about 35 minutes.

▶ Transfer artichokes, thyme, and garlic to a platter. Add remaining ¾ cup water to pot and deglaze by boiling over high heat, stirring and scraping up brown bits, 1 minute. Pour pan juices (they will be dark) into a small bowl and stir in extra-virgin olive oil and remaining ½ teaspoon salt. Squeeze pulp from 2 of garlic cloves into juices and mash into sauce with a fork.

▶ Divide artichokes and remaining garlic cloves among six plates and drizzle with sauce. Garlic cloves can be peeled and spread on crusty bread.

**COOKS' NOTE:** Trimmed artichokes can be kept chilled in lemon water for 8 hours.

# Asparagus, Peas, and Basil

*Adapted from Ursula Ferrigno*

Serves **6** | Active time: **30 minutes** | Start to finish: **30 minutes**

¼  **cup finely chopped shallots (about 2)**
3  **tablespoons unsalted butter**
2  **pounds asparagus, trimmed and cut into 1-inch pieces**
2½  **cups (12 ounces) shelled fresh peas (1¾ pounds in pods) or 1 (10-ounce) package thawed frozen peas**
   **Fine sea salt**
¼  **teaspoon black pepper**
   **Handful of torn fresh basil leaves (about ¾ cup)**

▶ Cook shallots in butter in a 12-inch heavy skillet over medium heat, stirring frequently, until just tender, about 4 minutes.

▶ Stir in asparagus, peas, ½ teaspoon sea salt, and pepper, then seal skillet with foil. Cook over medium heat until vegetables are tender but still slightly al dente, about 8 minutes. Stir in basil and sea salt to taste.

**COOKS' NOTE:** The peas can be shelled and asparagus cut 1 day ahead and chilled, covered.

This recipe is the perfect illustration of the "What grows together, goes together" maxim. Spring vegetables and herbs need only the most restrained treatment—a quick sauté with a little butter and shallot—to harmonize beautifully.

# Fennel, Frisée, and Escarole Salad

*Adapted from Tony Oltranti*

Serves 8 | Active time: **20 minutes** | Start to finish: **20 minutes**

This refreshing salad serves as a palate cleanser before dessert. Lemon juice amplifies the acidity of red-wine vinegar in a bright shallot vinaigrette, and Parmesan curls add a salty, nutty richness

3 tablespoons minced shallot
2 tablespoons fresh lemon juice
1 teaspoon red-wine vinegar, or to taste
½ teaspoon fine sea salt
½ teaspoon black pepper
1 small head escarole (¾ pound), torn into bite-size pieces
1 small head frisée (¾ pound), torn into bite-size pieces
1 small fennel bulb, quartered and thinly sliced or shaved with an adjustable-blade slicer
¼ cup fine-quality extra-virgin olive oil
1 (½-pound) piece Parmigiano-Reggiano

▶ Stir together shallot, lemon juice, vinegar, sea salt, and pepper in a small bowl. Let stand for 5 minutes. Meanwhile, toss together greens and fennel in a salad bowl.

▶ Whisk oil into shallot mixture, then toss with salad. Top with shaved Parmesan.

# Roasted Fennel and Baby Carrots

Serves 6 | Active time: 15 minutes | Start to finish: 45 minutes

Both fennel slices and baby carrots—not the fat nubs sold in bags, but the honest-to-goodness baby ones—respond to a bit of moisture when roasting. Our trick of starting them with a little water in the pan before uncovering and letting them caramelize is the difference between juicy and leathery roasted vegetables.

- 6 bunches baby carrots, peeled and trimmed, leaving ½ inch of stems intact
- 2 medium fennel bulbs, stalks discarded and bulbs cut into ½-inch-thick wedges
- 3 tablespoons olive oil
- 3 tablespoons water
- 1 teaspoon fennel seeds
- ¾ teaspoon salt
- ¼ teaspoon black pepper

▸ Preheat oven to 450°F, with racks in upper and lower thirds.

▸ Toss carrots and fennel with olive oil, water, fennel seeds, salt, and pepper and arrange in one layer on an 18-by-13-inch baking sheet. Cover pan with foil and roast vegetables in lower third of oven for 10 minutes, then uncover and roast, turning occasionally, 10 minutes more. Switch pan to upper third of oven and roast until vegetables are tender and browned, about 10 minutes more.

# Glazed Pearl Onions

Serves **8** | Active time: **25 minutes** | Start to finish: **50 minutes**

To lessen the tiresome peeling that tiny pearl onions require, we replaced some of them with red grapes—a shortcut that pays delicious dividends. The grapes' juicy pop plays nicely against many meat dishes, and a vinegar glaze contributes a winey complexity, tying the flavors together.

20   **ounces red pearl onions**
⅓   **cup sherry or red wine vinegar**
¼   **cup water**
2   **tablespoons sugar**
1   **tablespoon unsalted butter**
1   **Turkish or ½ California bay leaf**
½   **teaspoon salt**
¼   **teaspoon black pepper**
1½   **cups seedless red grapes (about ½ pound)**

▶ Preheat oven to 425°F.

▶ Blanch unpeeled pearl onions in boiling water for 2 minutes. Drain and transfer to an ice bath to stop cooking. Peel onions and trim off root ends, keeping onion intact.

▶ Bring onions, vinegar, and water to a simmer in an ovenproof 12-inch heavy skillet with sugar, butter, bay leaf, salt, and pepper, stirring until sugar has dissolved. Cover and simmer for 3 minutes.

▶ Uncover skillet and transfer to oven. Roast, stirring once or twice, until most of liquid has evaporated, 15 to 18 minutes. Stir in grapes and roast, stirring once or twice, until liquid glazes onions and grapes, 5 to 8 minutes. Discard bay leaf.

# Broccoli Rabe with Sweet Italian Sausage

*Adapted from Tony Oltranti*

**Serves 8** | **Active time: 30 minutes** | **Start to finish: 30 minutes**

The classic combination of bitter greens and sweet sausage is a warming and comforting dish that has been made for generations.

3 **pounds broccoli rabe (about 3 medium bunches), trimmed**

**Salt**

1½ **pounds sweet Italian sausage links, cut into 1-inch pieces**

5 **tablespoons extra-virgin olive oil**

5 **garlic cloves, chopped**

▶ Cut broccoli rabe into 3-inch-long pieces. Cook in a large pot of well-salted boiling water, uncovered, until tender, about 5 minutes. Drain, then rinse under cold water to stop cooking. Squeeze out excess water from handfuls of broccoli rabe, then separate.

▶ Meanwhile, preheat broiler.

▶ Broil sausage on a baking sheet 3 to 4 inches from heat, turning occasionally, until cooked through, about 5 minutes. Keep warm, covered.

▶ While sausage broils, heat oil in a 12-inch heavy skillet over medium-high heat until it shimmers, then cook garlic, stirring, until fragrant but not browned, about 1 minute.

▶ Add broccoli rabe and sauté until heated through, about 4 minutes. Stir in sausage.

**COOKS' NOTE:** The broccoli rabe can be boiled 1 day ahead and chilled.

# Carrots with Shallots, Sage, and Thyme

Serves **6 to 8** | Active time: **25 minutes** | Start to finish: **25 minutes**

Braised in chicken broth and combined with shallots and fresh herbs, these carrots make a stunning addition to the table— especially when you take advantage of the different-colored varieties found at farmers' markets.

3  **pounds carrots, peeled**
1  **cup chicken stock or reduced-sodium chicken broth**
   **Salt and black pepper**
½  **pound shallots, thinly sliced**
4  **tablespoons (½ stick) unsalted butter**
¼  **cup chopped fresh sage**
1  **tablespoon finely chopped fresh thyme**
¼  **teaspoon grated nutmeg**

▶ Cut carrots into 3-by-½-inch sticks.
▶ Bring stock to a boil with ¾ teaspoon salt and ½ teaspoon pepper in a 12-inch heavy skillet. Add carrots and simmer, covered, until just tender, about 15 minutes.
▶ Remove lid and boil until most of liquid has evaporated, about 5 minutes. Transfer carrots to a bowl and wipe out skillet.
▶ Cook shallots in butter with ½ teaspoon each salt and pepper in skillet over medium heat, stirring occasionally, until deep golden, about 6 minutes.
▶ Add sage, thyme, and nutmeg and cook, stirring, until very fragrant, 1 to 2 minutes.
▶ Remove from heat and return carrots to skillet, tossing to coat. Season with salt and pepper.

**COOKS' NOTE:** The carrots can be made 1 day ahead and chilled. Reheat over low heat.

KITCHEN TIP
## A CARROT A DAY . . .

Multicolored "rainbow" carrots are the darlings of chefs and food stylists, but their beauty is more than skin deep. It turns out that the various colors—yellow, red, purple, white—are each a rich source of different forms of carotene as well as healthful phytochemicals. Another little known fact: It's better to cook your carrots than eat them raw, because cooking breaks down the thick cell walls, making the nutrients more available to your body. What's more, carrots cooked whole and then cut up for eating have 25 percent more of an anti-cancer compound than those cut up before cooking, according to a study done at Newcastle University in England.

# Grilled Herbed Potatoes

Serves **4** | Active time: **20 minutes** | Start to finish: **25 minutes**

2 **pounds large Yukon Gold or other yellow-fleshed potatoes**
¼ **cup chopped mixed fresh herbs, such as parsley, chives, rosemary, and oregano**
2 **garlic cloves, smashed**
⅓ **cup extra-virgin olive oil**
**Salt and black pepper**
1 **lemon wedge, plus additional for serving**

▸ Prepare a gas grill for direct-heat cooking over medium-high heat; see page 11.
▸ Cut potatoes into ½-inch-thick slices and cook in a large pot of well-salted boiling water for 10 minutes (potatoes will not be cooked through).
▸ Meanwhile, stir together herbs, garlic, oil, ½ teaspoon salt, and ¼ teaspoon pepper in a large shallow dish.
▸ Drain potatoes well and transfer to herb oil, tossing gently to coat.
▸ Transfer potatoes to grill, letting excess oil drip into dish (reserve oil in dish). Grill potatoes, covered, turning once or twice, until tender, about 5 minutes total. Return potatoes to dish and toss again with herb oil. Squeeze lemon wedge over potatoes. Season with salt and serve with additional lemon wedges.

**COOKS' NOTE:** The potatoes can be cooked in a hot grill pan, 10 to 12 minutes.

Tuscan cooking revolves around the hearth and grill, and these *patate alla griglia* illustrate how well potatoes take to a quick bath in herbed oil and a turn over hot coals.

# Sautéed Greens

Serves **4** | Active time: **40 minutes** | Start to finish: **40 minutes**

Many of the greens that Italians love—escarole, chicory, broccoli rabe—have a bitter edge, but Italians know that blanching the greens first allows their sweetness to emerge.

2 **pounds dark leafy greens**
  **Salt**
3–4 **tablespoons extra-virgin olive oil**
3 **garlic cloves, finely chopped**
¼ **teaspoon hot red-pepper flakes**

▶ Trim the tough stems of the greens, then chop the leaves; wash and drain. Cook in a large pot of salted boiling water until just tender, 5 to 10 minutes. Drain, pressing out excess water.

▶ Heat the oil in a large heavy skillet over medium heat until it shimmers, then sauté the garlic cloves, with the hot pepper flakes until garlic is pale golden. Stir in greens with salt to taste, then sauté over medium-high heat until most liquid is evaporated.

# Butternut Squash with Shallots and Sage

Serves **4** | Active time: **20 minutes** | Start to finish: **25 minutes**

Fresh sage and a splash of balsamic vinegar transform succulent butternut squash and tender shallots into a beautifully balanced dish.

2 tablespoons olive oil

3 shallots, halved lengthwise and thinly sliced (¾ cup)

1 (1¾-pound) butternut squash, peeled, halved lengthwise, seeded, and cut into ½-inch cubes (4 cups)

½ cup reduced-sodium chicken broth or water

1 tablespoon packed brown sugar

½ teaspoon finely chopped fresh sage

 Salt

1 teaspoon balsamic vinegar

 Black pepper

▶ Heat oil in a 12-inch heavy skillet over medium heat until it shimmers, then cook shallots and squash, stirring, until shallots are softened, about 5 minutes.

▶ Add broth, brown sugar, sage, and ½ teaspoon salt, stirring until sugar is dissolved. Simmer, covered, stirring occasionally, until squash is tender, 8 to 10 minutes. Remove from heat and stir in vinegar, and salt and pepper to taste.

# Turnip Gratin

*Adapted from Holly Smith*

**Serves 6** | **Active time: 20 minutes** | **Start to finish: 1 hour**

Pan-roasting gives these paper-thin slices of turnip—a study in richness and lightness—a delicate, sweet taste.

2 tablespoons unsalted butter

2½ pounds medium turnips, trimmed and left unpeeled

1 tablespoon chopped fresh thyme

½ tablespoon chopped fresh savory

1½ teaspoons kosher salt

Rounded ⅛ teaspoon cayenne

1 cup heavy cream

1 cup grated Parmigiano-Reggiano (use a Microplane)

**SPECIAL EQUIPMENT**

Adjustable-blade slicer

▶ Preheat oven to 450°F, with rack in middle.

▶ Melt butter in an ovenproof 12-inch heavy skillet, then cool.

▶ Slice turnips paper-thin with slicer, then arrange one third of slices, overlapping tightly, in skillet, keeping remaining slices covered with dampened paper towels. Sprinkle with about a third of thyme, savory, salt, and cayenne. Make two more layers.

▶ Cook, covered, over medium heat until underside is browned, about 10 minutes. Add cream and cook, covered, until center is tender, 20 to 25 minutes.

▶ Sprinkle evenly with cheese, then bake, uncovered, until golden and bubbling, 10 to 15 minutes. Let stand for 5 minutes before serving.

**KITCHEN TIP**

## SHOPPING FOR TURNIPS

Although turnips are in supermarkets year round, the best time to buy them is in the fall and the spring, when they are just dug from the earth. If you have access to a farmers' market, make a beeline there because the fresher the turnip, the sweeter it is. Look for pearly white orbs about 2 inches in diameter, with bright purple shoulders. They should feel firm and heavy for their size. Attached greens are a plus because they denote fresh-ness and are delicious cooked (see page 131). Cut off the greens when you get home, and store roots and greens in separate plastic bags in the crisper drawer of your fridge. Although young turnips would be delightful, more mature turnips will also be transformed by the cream and cheese into a fabulous side dish.

# White Beans with Roasted Tomatoes

Serves 8 | Active time: **1 hour** | Start to finish: **9¼ hours**

This combination of white beans, tomatoes, and *cipolline* is exceptionally delicious. Letting your tomatoes cook to the point where they become caramelized and start to fall apart adds a layer of deep flavor to the dish.

**KITCHEN TIP**
## BEAN CHOICES

Beans are a crucial element of the Italian diet. The Tuscans are so fond of them that they are often referred to as *mangiafagioli*, or bean-eaters. Cannellini are probably the best-known Italian white bean, but if you can't find them, feel free to substitute other varieties such as Great Northerns, pea beans, or even dried limas. The older the bean, the longer it takes to cook, so it's best to shop for them in places with high turnover. Or shop online for heirloom varieties; an excellent source is ranchogordo.com.

### FOR BEANS

- 1 **pound dried cannellini beans (2 cups), picked over and rinsed**
- 1 **pound *cipolline* or small boiling onions (left unpeeled)**
- 1½ **teaspoons salt, or to taste**

### FOR TOMATOES

- 2 **pounds large tomatoes, cored and halved crosswise**
- 1 **pound cherry tomatoes (preferably mixed colors; 4 cups)**
- 1 **teaspoon salt (preferably sea salt)**
- 1 **teaspoon sugar**
- ½ **cup extra-virgin olive oil**
- ¼ **cup torn fresh basil leaves**

▶ **COOK BEANS:** Generously cover beans with cold water in a bowl and soak at room temperature for at least 8 hours or quick-soak (see Cooks' Note). Drain well in a colander.

▶ Blanch onions in well-salted boiling water for 1 minute, then drain and peel.

▶ Cover beans with cold water by about 1 inch in a 5- to 6-quart pot and bring to a boil. Add onions and simmer, partially covered, skimming froth as necessary, until beans and onions are tender, 40 minutes to 1 hour. Stir in salt and let stand (in cooking liquid), uncovered.

▶ **ROAST TOMATOES WHILE BEANS ARE COOKING:** Preheat oven to 500°F, with rack in upper third.

▶ Toss tomato halves and cherry tomatoes with salt, sugar, and oil in a shallow 3-quart baking dish, then arrange tomato halves cut sides up. Roast tomatoes, uncovered, until large tomatoes are very tender with brown patches and cherry tomatoes are falling apart, 35 to 50 minutes.

▶ **ASSEMBLE DISH:** Transfer warm beans and onions with a slotted spoon to a deep large platter. Arrange tomatoes decoratively on top of beans and pour tomato juices on top. Sprinkle with basil leaves.

**COOKS' NOTES:** The beans can be cooked 1 day ahead. Cool in liquid, uncovered, then chill, covered. Reheat in liquid over low heat, covered, stirring occasionally, before assembling the dish.

To quick-soak beans, cover the dried beans with triple their volume of cold water in a large saucepan. Bring to a boil and cook, uncovered, over medium heat for 2 minutes. Remove from the heat and soak the beans, covered, for 1 hour.

The tomatoes can be roasted 2 hours ahead and kept, uncovered, at room temperature. Reheat, loosely covered with foil, in a 350°F oven until heated through, 15 to 20 minutes.

# Panna Cotta with Lemon-Thyme Peaches

**Serves 4** | Active time: **20 minutes** | Start to finish: **8½ hours**

A pudding-soft honey and almond panna cotta provides a gentle base for peaches that have been macerated with lemon thyme just long enough to meld and soften.

**FOR PANNA COTTA**

| | |
|---|---|
| 1¼ | **teaspoons unflavored gelatin (from a ¼-ounce envelope)** |
| 2 | **tablespoons water** |
| 1¼ | **cups heavy cream** |
| ⅛ | **teaspoon salt** |
| 1 | **cup plain low-fat yogurt** |
| ¼ | **cup mild honey** |
| ⅛ | **teaspoon pure almond extract** |

**FOR PEACHES**

| | |
|---|---|
| 1½ | **tablespoons fresh lemon thyme leaves** |
| 1 | **tablespoon sugar** |
| 3 | **peaches, peeled if desired, pitted, and thinly sliced** |

▶ **MAKE PANNA COTTA:** Sprinkle gelatin over water in a small heavy saucepan and let stand for 1 minute to soften. Stir in cream and salt, then heat gently over medium-low heat, stirring, until gelatin has dissolved.

▶ Whisk together yogurt, honey, and almond extract, then whisk in cream mixture.

▶ Pour mixture into four small bowls and chill, covered, until set, at least 8 hours.

▶ **PREPARE PEACHES:** Mince lemon thyme with sugar, then toss with peaches. Let macerate, stirring occasionally, at room temperature for 20 minutes. While peaches macerate, let panna cotta stand at room temperature.

▶ **TO SERVE:** Top bowls of panna cotta with peaches and their juice. Drizzle with additional honey if desired.

**COOKS' NOTE:** The panna cotta can be chilled for up to 3 days.

**KITCHEN TIP**

## UNMOLDING PANNA COTTA

The translation from Italian—"cooked cream"—doesn't begin to convey how luscious the gently gelled sweet cream mixture called panna cotta is. The amount of gelatin determines how tender the results will be. If you don't plan to unmold the dessert, you can play a bit with the gelatin, lowering it to a point where the panna cotta is set so softly that it holds its shape on a spoon but dissolves into a puddle on your tongue, like this one. If you want to try molded versions, be sure to lightly oil your molds first and chill the panna cotta well, at least 6 hours. When it's time to turn them out, dip each mold for about 10 seconds in a bowl of warm water, then dry off the bottom before inverting it onto a plate.

# Simple Almond Biscotti

*Adapted from Tony Oltranti*

Makes **42** | Active time: **20 minutes** | Start to finish: **2½ hours**

These biscotti are among the best we've had. Starting with a lot of almonds in a sticky dough, the recipe makes crunchy cookies that taste even better a day or two later—if they last that long.

1  **cup sugar**

8  **tablespoons (1 stick) unsalted butter, melted**

3  **tablespoons brandy**

2  **teaspoons pure almond extract**

1  **teaspoon pure vanilla extract**

1  **cup whole almonds with skin, lightly toasted, cooled, and coarsely chopped**

3  **large eggs**

2¾  **cups all-purpose flour**

1½  **teaspoons baking powder**

¼  **teaspoon salt**

▶ Stir together sugar, butter, brandy, and extracts in a large bowl, then stir in almonds and eggs. Stir in flour, baking powder, and salt until just combined.

▶ Chill dough, covered, for 30 minutes.

▶ Preheat oven to 350°F, with rack in middle.

▶ Using moistened hands, halve dough and form 2 (16-by-2-inch) loaves on an ungreased large baking sheet.

▶ Bake until pale golden, about 30 minutes. Carefully transfer loaves to a rack and cool for 15 minutes.

▶ Cut loaves into ¾-inch slices with a serrated knife.

▶ Arrange biscotti, cut side down, on a clean baking sheet and bake until golden, 20 to 25 minutes. Transfer to rack to cool.

# Chewy Amaretti Sandwich Cookies

The *amaretti* cookies most Americans are familiar with are deep golden brown and extremely crisp. These three-ingredient wonders are the total opposite: pale, soft, and chewy, not to mention truly addictive.

Makes **4 dozen** | Active time: **20 minutes** | Start to finish: **1 hour**

1  **(7-ounce) tube pure almond paste (not marzipan; ¾ cup)**
1  **cup sugar**
2  **large egg whites, at room temperature for 30 minutes**

SPECIAL EQUIPMENT
   **Pastry bag with a ⅜-inch plain tip**

▶ Preheat oven to 300°F, with racks in upper and lower thirds. Line two large (18-by-13-inch) baking sheets with parchment paper.

▶ Pulse almond paste and sugar in a food processor until broken up, then add egg whites and pulse until smooth. Transfer to pastry bag and pipe ¾-inch rounds (⅓-inch high) about ¾ inch apart in pans. Dip a fingertip in water and gently tamp down any peaks.

▶ Bake, rotating and switching position of pans halfway through, until golden and puffed, 15 to 18 minutes.

▶ Wearing an oven mitt, rest one pan in sink at an angle. Lift top edge of parchment and slowly pour about ¼ cup water between parchment and baking sheet so that all of parchment is lightly moistened (water will steam on pan, moistening bottom of cookies to help them stick together later). Repeat with remaining baking sheet. Cool cookies in pans on racks.

▶ Peel cookies from parchment and sandwich bottoms of cookies together.

**COOKS' NOTE:** The cookies can be kept in an airtight container at room temperature for 1 day or frozen for up to 1 month.

# Panettone Bread Pudding

*Adapted from Tony Oltranti*

**Serves 8** | Active time: **30 minutes** | Start to finish: **2 hours**

Store-bought panettone is the foundation of this raisin and bread pudding. Because the bread is so eggy, it bakes into an extra-silky custard that contrasts with a generous expanse of buttery golden brown crispness on top. (Using a shallow pan is key.)

½   **cup golden raisins**
¼   **cup brandy, heated**
4   **tablespoons (½ stick) unsalted butter, softened**
1   **pound panettone, sliced 1-inch thick**
¾   **cup sugar**
3   **large eggs, lightly beaten**
2½  **cups half-and-half**
2   **tablespoons pure vanilla extract**
**ACCOMPANIMENT**
    **Lightly whipped heavy cream**

▶ Soak raisins in hot brandy for 15 minutes, then drain (discard brandy or reserve for making Simple Almond Biscotti, page 142).

▶ Meanwhile, butter panettone on both sides and cook in batches in a large heavy skillet over medium heat until golden on both sides.

▶ Whisk together remaining ingredients. Tear panettone into bite-size pieces and spread evenly in a buttered 13-by-9-inch baking dish. Scatter raisins over top, then pour in egg mixture. Let stand for 30 minutes.

▶ Preheat oven to 350°F, with rack in middle.

▶ Bake until pudding is deep golden and just set, 35 to 40 minutes. Serve warm or at room temperature, with whipped cream.

**COOKS' NOTE:** The bread pudding can be made 2 days ahead and chilled. Reheat before serving.

# Easy Chocolate Nemesis

*Adapted from Rose Gray and Ruth Rogers*

**Serves 6** | **Active time: 35 minutes** | **Start to finish: 3¾ hours**

This chocolate confection, slowly baked in a hot water bath, comes out somewhere between an Italian *budino* (pudding) and the most decadent flourless chocolate cake you've ever eaten.

**KITCHEN TIP**

### DON'T CHEAT ON THE CHOCOLATE

Shopping for baking chocolate has gotten much easier since manufacturers began labeling bittersweet chocolate with the percentage of cocoa solids. It's a real boon for the consumer because loose federal regulations mean the amount of cacao in bittersweet can vary widely; it needs only a minimum of 35 percent. Many commercial brands range from 50 to 60 percent. If a recipe (such as Easy Chocolate Nemesis) calls for a specific percentage, resist the temptation to substitute chocolate with less (60%), or more (85%) cocoa solids because the texture of the cake will not be the same.

16 tablespoons (2 sticks) unsalted butter, plus additional for greasing pan

12 ounces fine-quality bittersweet chocolate (70% cacao), coarsely chopped

5 large eggs

1 cup sugar

7 tablespoons water

**SPECIAL EQUIPMENT**

10-by-2-inch round cake pan (not a springform); parchment paper

**ACCOMPANIMENT**

Mascarpone or whipped cream

▶ Preheat oven to 300°F, with rack in middle. Butter a cake pan and line bottom with a round of parchment paper, then butter parchment.

▶ Melt chocolate with butter in a large metal bowl set over a pan of barely simmering water, stirring occasionally, until just smooth, then remove from heat.

▶ Beat together eggs and ⅓ cup sugar in a large bowl with an electric mixer at high speed until tripled in volume and thick enough to form a ribbon that takes 2 seconds to dissolve when beater is lifted, about 5 minutes in a standing mixer or 10 minutes with a handheld.

▶ Heat remaining ⅔ cup sugar and 7 tablespoons water in a small saucepan over medium-low heat, stirring, until sugar is dissolved and syrup is clear, about 2 minutes. Pour hot syrup into melted chocolate, stirring to combine, then cool 10 minutes.

▶ Add chocolate syrup, a little at a time, to egg mixture, beating at medium speed, and continue to beat until just incorporated, then pour batter into cake pan.

▶ Put cake pan into a roasting pan lined with a kitchen towel, then add enough boiling-hot water to reach about three quarters of the way up side of cake pan. Bake until just set, 50 minutes to 1 hour.

▶ Cool cake completely in water bath before unmolding, at least 2 hours. Run a thin knife around edge of cake pan to loosen if necessary, then invert a flat platter over pan and flip cake onto platter. Carefully peel off parchment. Serve with mascarpone or whipped cream.

**COOKS' NOTE:** The cake can be made 6 hours ahead and kept in the pan, covered, at room temperature.

# Tiramisu

Serves **8 to 10** | Active time: **30 minutes** | Start to finish: **7 hours**

A cloud of featherlight zabaglione mixed with mascarpone and whipped cream is layered with Italian ladyfingers softened by their dip in liqueur-spiked espresso. This tiramisu (Italian for "pick-me-up") is a dream of a dessert—not least because it's so easy to put together.

- 2 cups boiling water
- 3 tablespoons instant-espresso powder (see Cooks' Note)
- ½ cup plus 1 tablespoon sugar
- 3 tablespoons Tia Maria (coffee liqueur)
- 4 large egg yolks
- ⅓ cup dry Marsala
- 1 pound mascarpone (2½ cups; see page 184)
- 1 cup chilled heavy cream
- 36 *savoiardi* (crisp Italian ladyfinger biscuits; from two 7-ounce packages)
- Unsweetened cocoa powder for dusting

**SPECIAL EQUIPMENT**
13-by-9-by-3-inch baking dish

▶ Stir together water, espresso powder, 1 tablespoon sugar, and Tia Maria in a shallow bowl until sugar dissolves; cool.

▶ Beat egg yolks, Marsala, and remaining ½ cup sugar in a metal bowl set over a saucepan of barely simmering water using a whisk or handheld electric mixer until tripled in volume, 5 to 8 minutes. Remove bowl from heat. Beat in mascarpone until just combined.

▶ Beat cream in a large bowl until it holds stiff peaks.

▶ Fold mascarpone mixture into whipped cream gently but thoroughly.

▶ Dipping both sides of each ladyfinger into coffee mixture, line bottom of baking dish with 18 ladyfingers in 3 rows, trimming edges to fit if necessary. Spread half of mascarpone filling on top. Dip remaining 18 ladyfingers in coffee and arrange over filling in dish.

▶ Spread remaining mascarpone filling on top and dust with cocoa. Chill, covered, at least 6 hours.

▶ Let tiramisu stand at room temperature for 30 minutes before serving, then dust with more cocoa.

**COOKS' NOTES:** You can substitute 2 cups freshly brewed espresso for the water and instant-espresso powder.

The tiramisu can be chilled for up to 2 days.

The yolks in this dessert may not be fully cooked.

# Fig Crostata

Serves **8** | Active time: **1 hour** | Start to finish: **3½ hours**

A rich filling is studded with walnuts and imbued with citrusy notes of orange, then packaged between a crust and a lattice top, both made from the cookie-like pastry dough known in Italy as *pasta frolla*.

- 2 **cups all-purpose flour**
- ¼ **cup granulated sugar, plus additional for sprinkling**
- ½ **teaspoon salt**
- 12 **tablespoons (1½ sticks) cold unsalted butter, cut into ½-inch cubes**
- 2 **large egg yolks**
- 1 **teaspoon pure vanilla extract**
- 1 **tablespoon cold water**

**FOR FIG FILLING**

- 12 **ounces soft dried figs (preferably Calmyrna), stemmed and coarsely chopped**
- 1¼ **cups water**
- 1 **cup fresh orange juice**
- ½ **cup packed dark brown sugar**
- 8 **tablespoons (1 stick) unsalted butter, melted and cooled**
- 3 **large eggs, lightly beaten**
- 1 **teaspoon pure vanilla extract**
- 1 **teaspoon grated orange zest**
- 1½ **cups walnuts (6 ounces), coarsely chopped**

**SPECIAL EQUIPMENT**

**9-inch springform pan**

**ACCOMPANIMENT**

**Mascarpone**

▶ **MAKE PASTRY DOUGH:** Blend together flour, sugar, salt, and butter in a bowl with your fingertips or a pastry blender (or pulse in a food processor) just until mixture resembles coarse meal with some roughly pea-size butter lumps. Add yolks, vanilla, and water and gently stir with a fork (or pulse) until incorporated and dough begins to form large clumps.

► Turn out dough onto a lightly floured surface and divide into 4 portions. With heel of your hand, smear each portion once or twice in a forward motion to help distribute fat. Gather all dough together (using a pastry scraper if you have one), then divide dough in half and form each half into a 5- to 6-inch disk. Chill, wrapped in plastic wrap, until firm, at least 1 hour.

► **MAKE FIG FILLING WHILE DOUGH CHILLS:** Simmer figs, water, orange juice, and brown sugar in a medium saucepan, covered, stirring occasionally, until figs are soft and mixture is reduced to about 2 cups, 15 to 20 minutes. Pulse in a food processor until finely chopped (mixture should not be smooth). Transfer to a large bowl and cool slightly. Stir in butter, eggs, vanilla, zest, and walnuts.

► **MAKE TART SHELL:** Preheat oven to 350°F, with rack in middle. Generously butter springform pan.

► Roll out 1 portion of dough between 2 sheets of parchment paper into a 12-inch round (dough will be soft; chill or freeze briefly if it becomes difficult to work with). Peel off top sheet of parchment and carefully invert dough into pan. (Dough will tear easily but can be patched together with your fingers.) Press dough onto bottom and 1 inch up side of pan, then trim excess. Chill tart shell until ready to assemble crostata.

► Roll out remaining dough between two sheets of parchment paper into a 12-inch round. Peel off top sheet of parchment, then cut dough into 10 (1-inch-wide) strips and slide (still on parchment) onto a tray. Chill until firm, about 10 minutes.

► **ASSEMBLE CROSTATA:** Spread fig filling in shell. Arrange 5 strips of dough 1 inch apart on filling. Arrange remaining 5 strips 1 inch apart across first strips to form a lattice. Trim edges of strips flush with edge of shell. Sprinkle crostata with sugar.

► Bake until filling is slightly puffed and pastry is pale golden, about 30 minutes. Cool completely, then remove side of pan. Serve crostata with mascarpone.

**COOKS' NOTES:** The crostata can be made 1 day ahead and kept at room temperature.

The dough can be chilled for up to 3 days.

# Pear, Apple, and Quince Crostata

*Adapted from Jonathan Waxman*

Serves **6 to 8** | Active time: **1 hour** | Start to finish: **5 hours**

Not too rich or too sweet, this crostata achieves a light texture with ample butter. Pears and apples—cushioned in a brown sugar filling—are lushly flavored but tempered with a subtle note of quince.

2 **firm-ripe pears (1 pound total)**
2 **apples (preferably Fuji or Gala; 1 pound total)**
1 **quince (½ pound)**
½ **cup granulated sugar**
3 **tablespoons fresh lemon juice**
1 **tablespoon peeled, finely chopped fresh ginger**
1 **(3-inch) cinnamon stick**
4 **whole cloves**
2 **tablespoons apple cider**

**FOR PASTRY SHELL**

2 **cups all-purpose flour**
1 **teaspoon kosher salt**
3 **tablespoons granulated sugar**
16 **tablespoons (2 sticks) cold unsalted butter, cut into ½-inch cubes**
6–8 **tablespoons ice water**
1 **large egg, lightly beaten**

**FOR BROWN SUGAR FILLING**

1 **stick (8 tablespoons) unsalted butter, softened**
½ **cup packed light brown sugar**
½ **cup confectioners' sugar**
2 **large eggs**
1 **teaspoon vanilla**
¼ **cup all-purpose flour**
**Pinch of salt**

**SPECIAL EQUIPMENT**

**Pastry or bench scraper; 11-inch round fluted tart pan (1¼ inches deep) with removable bottom**

▶ **MAKE ROASTED FRUIT:** Preheat oven to 375°, with rack in middle.

▶ Peel, quarter, and core pears, apples, and quince, then cut into 1-inch chunks. Toss fruit with sugar, lemon juice, ginger, cinnamon stick, cloves, and 1 tablespoon apple cider in a bowl. Transfer to a large (18-by-13-inch) baking sheet and roast, stirring once or twice, until fruit is very soft and caramelized, 1 to 1¼ hours.

▸ Remove from oven and add remaining tablespoon apple cider, scraping up caramelized juices from bottom of baking pan. Discard cinnamon stick and cloves. Cool in pan on a rack, about 45 minutes.

▸ **MAKE PASTRY SHELL WHILE FRUIT ROASTS:** Whisk together flour, salt, and 2 tablespoons sugar in a large bowl. Blend in butter with your fingertips or a pastry blender (or pulse in a food processor) until mixture resembles coarse meal with some roughly pea-size butter lumps. Drizzle evenly with 6 tablespoons ice water and gently stir with a fork (or pulse) until incorporated.

▸ Squeeze a small handful: If dough doesn't hold together, add more ice water to dough, 1 tablespoon at a time, stirring (or pulsing) until just combined. (Do not overwork mixture, or pastry will be tough.)

▸ Turn out dough onto a lightly floured surface and divide into 6 portions. With heel of your hand, smear each portion once or twice in a forward motion to help distribute fat. Gather all of dough together with scraper and press into a ball, then flatten into a disk. Chill dough, wrapped tightly in plastic wrap, until firm, at least 1 hour.

▸ Roll out dough on a lightly floured surface with a lightly floured rolling pin into a 14-inch round, then fit into tart pan (do not trim overhang).

▸ **MAKE BROWN SUGAR FILLING:** Put a large baking sheet in middle of oven and preheat oven to 375°F.

▸ Beat together butter and sugars in a large bowl using an electric mixer at high speed until pale and fluffy, about 2 minutes. Add eggs 1 at a time, beating well after each addition, then beat in vanilla. Reduce speed to low, then add flour and a pinch of salt and mix until just combined. Spread evenly in pastry shell.

▸ **ASSEMBLE AND BAKE PASTRY:** Scatter roasted fruit with juices over filling. Fold edge of pastry over filling to partially cover (center won't be covered). Pleat dough as necessary. Brush folded pastry edge lightly with egg and sprinkle with remaining tablespoon sugar.

▸ Bake on preheated baking sheet until filling is puffed and set and pastry is golden brown, 50 to 60 minutes. Cool to warm, about 1½ hours. Remove side of tart pan and slide crostata onto a plate.

**COOKS' NOTES:** The pastry dough can be chilled for up to 1 day.

The fruit can be roasted 1 day ahead and chilled, covered.

The crostata can be baked 6 hours ahead and kept (in the tart pan) at room temperature. Reheat if desired.

# Apricot Almond Macaroon Cake

Serves **6** | Active time: **45 minutes** | Start to finish: **2½ hours**

A crowd-pleasing dessert fit for a celebration: The tiers of this sweet-tart apricot almond cake are chewy with nuts and meringue, delicate with ruffled edges, and spirited with Amaretto-tinged mascarpone.

**FOR ALMOND MACAROON LAYERS**
- 12 **ounces sliced blanched almonds (3¾ cups) or blanched slivered almonds (2¾ cups)**
- 3⅓ **cups confectioners' sugar**
- 6 **large egg whites**
- ¼ **teaspoon salt**
- 6 **tablespoons granulated sugar**

**FOR APRICOT COMPOTE**
- 6 **ounces dried California/Pacific apricots (1½ cups), finely chopped**
- 1½ **cups water**
- 3 **tablespoons apricot preserves**

**FOR PRALINE ALMONDS**
- 1 **cup sliced blanched almonds (3 ounces)**
- ½ **cup confectioners' sugar**

**FOR MASCARPONE CREAM**
- 1½ **cups imported Italian mascarpone**
- ¼ **cup well-chilled heavy cream**
- ¼ **cup Disaronno Amaretto or other almond-flavored liqueur**

**SPECIAL EQUIPMENT**
**Parchment paper**

▶ **MAKE MACAROON LAYERS:** Trace 2 (8-inch) circles on 1 sheet of parchment paper and a third circle on second sheet. Turn sheets over and put on two baking sheets.

▶ Pulse almonds with 1⅓ cups confectioners' sugar in a food processor until very finely ground (mixture will resemble sand), 2 to 3 minutes. Transfer to a large bowl and sift in remaining 2 cups confectioners' sugar, then stir until combined well.

▶ Beat egg whites with salt in a large bowl with an electric mixer at medium speed until they just hold soft peaks. Add granulated sugar a little at a time, beating, then increase speed to high and continue to beat until whites hold stiff, glossy peaks, about 3 minutes.

▶ Stir whites into almond mixture until completely incorporated (batter will be thick), then divide evenly among traced circles on baking sheets (about 1⅔ cups per circle), smoothing into ½-inch-thick rounds. Let rounds stand, uncovered, at room temperature until tops are no longer sticky and a light crust forms, about 30 minutes.

▶ Preheat oven to 300°F, with racks in upper and lower thirds.

▶ Bake macaroon layers, switching position of baking sheets halfway through cooking, until macaroons are crisp and edges are just barely pale golden, about 25 minutes. Turn off oven and let macaroons stand in oven for 10 minutes. Cool completely on baking sheets on racks, about 1 hour.

▶ **MAKE COMPOTE WHILE MACAROON LAYERS BAKE:** Simmer dried apricots in water in a 2- to 3-quart heavy saucepan, uncovered, over medium heat, stirring occasionally, until apricots are very soft

and most of liquid is evaporated, about 15 minutes. Stir in preserves, then cool completely.

▶ **MAKE PRALINE ALMONDS:** Heat almonds in a 12-inch dry heavy skillet over medium heat, stirring frequently, until almonds are hot but not yet colored, about 2 minutes. Add confectioners' sugar and continue cooking, stirring and tossing, until almonds are lightly toasted and sugar glaze is caramelized, about 3 minutes. Immediately transfer almonds to a large sheet of foil and spread into one layer with a fork. Cool completely.

▶ **MAKE MASCARPONE CREAM:** Just before serving, beat together mascarpone, heavy cream, and Amaretto with cleaned beaters at medium speed until thick and smooth, about 2 minutes. Reserve ¼ cup praline almonds, then fold remainder into cream.

▶ Put 1 macaroon layer on a platter and spread with ⅓ of compote (about ½ cup), then spread ¼ of mascarpone cream (about ¾ cup) on top. Make another layer with second macaroon in same manner. Top with remaining macaroon, remaining compote, and remaining cream (1½ cups), then sprinkle with reserved praline almonds.

**COOKS' NOTES:** The macaroon layers can be made 2 days ahead and kept in an airtight container, layered between parchment paper, at room temperature. Don't assemble this cake ahead or the crisp layers will get soggy.

The apricot compote can be made 5 days ahead and chilled, covered.

The praline almonds can be made 5 days ahead and kept in an airtight container at room temperature.

California or Pacific dried apricots are essential for this recipe—they have the tartness needed to balance the sweet filling and macaroon layers.

# Caramel Espresso Float

Serves **4** | Active time: **20 minutes** | Start to finish: **30 minutes**

This float was inspired by the Italian dessert *affogato al caffè*, which consists of ice cream that has been "drowned" in hot coffee.

6  tablespoons granulated sugar
2  cups water
¼  cup instant-espresso powder
2  cups ice cubes
½  cup chilled heavy cream
3  tablespoons confectioners' sugar
4  generous scoops good-quality
    vanilla ice cream (from 1 pint)
2  tablespoons chopped nuts, such as
    almonds or hazelnuts, toasted
3  tablespoons bittersweet chocolate
    shavings (made with a vegetable
    peeler)

▶ Cook granulated sugar in a dry 2- to 3-quart heavy saucepan over medium heat, undisturbed, until it begins to melt. Continue to cook, stirring occasionally with a fork, until sugar melts into a deep golden caramel. Remove from heat and carefully add 1 cup water (caramel will harden and steam vigorously). Cook over high heat, stirring, until caramel is dissolved, then remove pan from heat. Add espresso powder and stir until dissolved. Add remaining cup water and ice cubes and stir until espresso is cold. Discard any unmelted ice cubes.

▶ Beat cream with confectioners' sugar in a bowl with an electric mixer until it just holds soft peaks. Divide ice cream among four (8-ounce) glasses, then pour espresso over each serving and top with whipped cream, nuts, and chocolate shavings.

# CHAPTER 7

# BASICS

# Basic Tomato Sauce

Makes **6 cups** | Active time: **20 minutes** | Start to finish: **1 hour**

There's a subtle snobbery that says a sauce made with fresh tomatoes is superior—but that's crazy! Canned tomatoes are picked and packed at their peak, and you can't beat them for convenience. While some recipes keep you busy with lots of chopping, we love this straightforward version, which highlights the tomatoes with a little garlic and basil.

2 **(28-ounce) cans whole tomatoes in juice**
3 **tablespoons olive oil**
1 **medium onion, finely chopped**
4 **garlic cloves, finely chopped**
1 **teaspoon sugar**
  **Salt**
3 **tablespoons chopped fresh basil or parsley**

▶ Chop the tomatoes, reserving the juice. Heat the oil in a 5- to 6-quart heavy pot over medium-high heat until it shimmers, then sauté the onion until golden. Add the garlic and sauté until golden, about 1 minute.

▶ Add the tomatoes with their juice, sugar, and ¾ teaspoon salt and simmer, uncovered, stirring occasionally, until thickened, 30 to 35 minutes. Stir in the basil or parsley and remove from heat. Season with salt.

# Classic Pesto

Makes **1 cup; serves 4** | Active time: **15 minutes** | Start to finish: **15 minutes**

This nut-thickened paste of basil, garlic, and Parmigiano is the David that knocked the Goliath of spaghetti marinara on its head. Don't reserve it just for pasta: Slather on sandwiches in place of mayonnaise, or stir into soups for a hit of fresh herbal aroma.

- 2–3 **large garlic cloves**
  **Fine sea salt**
- ⅓ **cup pine nuts or walnuts**
- 2½ **cups packed fresh basil leaves**
- ½ **cup packed fresh flat-leaf parsley leaves**
- ⅓ **cup grated Parmigiano-Reggiano, plus more for serving**
- ⅓ **cup extra-virgin olive oil**
- 1 **pound linguine or spaghetti**
  **Black pepper**

▶ Mince and mash the garlic to a paste with ½ teaspoon salt. Pulse the pine nuts or walnuts in a food processor until finely ground. Add garlic paste, basil, and parsley to processor and pulse until finely chopped. Add Parmesan and oil and pulse to combine.

▶ To serve with pasta, put ¾ cup pesto in a large serving bowl. Cook linguine or spaghetti in a 6- to 8-quart pot of well-salted boiling water until al dente, then whisk enough cooking water—⅓ to ½ cup—into pesto to thin it to a sauce. Drain pasta and add to sauce, then toss well. Season with salt and pepper. Serve with additional grated Parmesan.

# Spaghetti Carbonara

Serves **4** | Active time: **40 minutes** | Start to finish: **40 minutes**

If authenticity is your passion, do as the Romans do and track down some *guanciale* (unsmoked cured hog jowl)—or failing that, pancetta—but rest assured that good old smoked bacon also makes an extremely satisfying version of this easy yet sophisticated sauce.

5 ounces *guanciale* (unsmoked cured hog jowl), pancetta, or bacon
1 medium onion, finely chopped
¼ cup dry white wine
1 pound spaghetti
3 large eggs
¾ cup grated Parmigiano-Reggiano
⅓ cup grated Pecorino Romano
¼ teaspoon salt
1 teaspoon coarsely ground black pepper

▶ Cut the *guanciale*, pancetta, or bacon into ⅓-inch dice, then cook in a deep 12-inch heavy skillet over medium heat, stirring, until fat begins to render, 1 to 2 minutes. Add the onion and cook, stirring occasionally, until golden, about 10 minutes. Add the wine and boil until reduced by half, 1 to 2 minutes.

▶ Cook the spaghetti in a 6- to 8-quart pot of well-salted boiling water until al dente.

▶ While pasta is cooking, whisk together the eggs, cheeses, salt, and pepper in a large bowl.

▶ Drain spaghetti in a colander and add to onion mixture, then toss with tongs over medium heat until coated. Transfer hot pasta to egg mixture and toss well (eggs will not be fully cooked). Serve immediately.

# Fettuccine Alfredo

Serves **4** | Active time: **10 minutes** | Start to finish: **20 minutes**

This creamy fettuccine is truly indulgent, and yet so simple. You'll be rewarded for using the very best pasta and Parmesan.

½ cup heavy cream
½ stick (4 tablespoons) unsalted butter, cut into pieces
¼ teaspoon salt
½ teaspoon black pepper
8–9 ounces dried egg fettuccine
⅓ cup grated Parmigiano-Reggiano

▶ Bring the cream and butter to a simmer with salt and pepper in a 12-inch heavy skillet over medium-low heat, then keep warm off heat, covered.
▶ Cook fettuccine in a 6- to 8-quart pot of well-salted boiling water until al dente. Reserve ½ cup cooking water, then drain pasta and add to skillet with ¼ cup reserved water and Parmesan; toss well. Add more cooking water if necessary.

# Aglio e Olio

Spaghetti with Garlic and Oil

**Serves 4** | **Active time: 45 minutes** | **Start to finish: 1 hour**

There's no simpler sauce for pasta in the Italian repertoire than garlic and oil. As easy as it is to make, it's also easy to screw up, so don't rush the cooking of the garlic in the oil. Let it color slowly, so you'll have more control over when to take it off the heat.

1½ **large heads garlic**

¼–½ **teaspoon hot pepper flakes**

4 **tablespoons extra-virgin olive oil, plus**
  **2–3 tablespoons for drizzling**

1 **pound spaghetti**

2 **teaspoons grated fresh lemon zest**

¼ **teaspoon salt**

½ **cup finely chopped fresh flat-leaf parsley**

▸ Separate the garlic into cloves and peel (don't crush). Thinly slice lengthwise as evenly as possible (you should have about 1 cup; peel and slice more if necessary). Cook garlic and hot pepper flakes in 4 tablespoons oil in a 12-inch heavy skillet over medium-low heat, stirring occasionally, until pale golden, 7 to 10 minutes. Remove skillet from heat (garlic will continue to cook in residual heat).

▸ Meanwhile, cook spaghetti until al dente; reserve 1 cup cooking water, then drain pasta and transfer to a serving bowl.

▸ Stir the lemon zest and salt into garlic oil in skillet, then pour mixture over hot pasta. Add parsley and drizzle 2 to 3 tablespoons more oil over pasta, then toss, adding some reserved cooking water to keep pasta moist.

# Fresh Egg Fettuccine

**Serves 12** | **Active time: 1¼ hours** | **Start to finish: 2¼ hours**

When you want a showstopper noodle—to accompany the Sunday Ragù (page 63) or any recipe—make your own. Although this flour, semolina, and egg mixture begins as a stiff dough, it cooks into beautiful, velvety fettuccine. A pasta machine makes this recipe easy and foolproof.

2  **cups unbleached all-purpose flour**
2  **cups semolina (sometimes called semolina flour)**
5  **large eggs, lightly beaten**
½  **teaspoon salt**
**SPECIAL EQUIPMENT**
   **Pasta machine**

▶ **MAKE DOUGH:** Whisk together flour and semolina, then mound on a large work surface (preferably wooden). Make a well in center and add eggs and salt to well. (Alternatively, put ingredients in a food processor.)

▶ Gradually stir enough flour into eggs (using a fork) to form a paste, pulling in flour closest to egg mixture and being careful not to make an opening in wall of well. Knead remaining flour into mixture with your hands to form a dough (it should be firm and not sticky).

▶ Knead dough until smooth and elastic, 8 to 10 minutes. (If using a processor, blend about 30 seconds total. If it doesn't come together, add 1 to 2 tablespoons water and blend.)

▶ Cover dough with an inverted bowl and let dough rest 1 hour to make rolling easier.

▶ **ROLL OUT PASTA:** Divide dough into 8 pieces, then flatten each piece into a rough rectangle and cover rectangles with an inverted large bowl. Set rollers of pasta machine on widest setting.

▶ Lightly dust 1 rectangle with flour and feed through rollers. (Keep remaining dough under bowl.) Fold rectangle in thirds and feed it, short end first, through rollers 7 or 8 more times, folding it in thirds each time and feeding short end through. Dust with flour if necessary to prevent sticking.

▶ Turn dial to next (narrower) setting and feed dough through rollers without folding. Continue to feed dough through rollers once at each setting, without folding, until you reach the second to narrowest setting. Dough will be a smooth sheet (about 36 inches long and 4 inches wide). Cut sheet in half crosswise.

▶ Lay sheets of dough on lightly floured baking sheets to dry until leathery but still pliable, about 15 minutes. (Alternatively, lightly dust pasta sheets with flour and hang over the backs of chairs to dry.) Roll out remaining pieces of dough in same manner.

▶ **CUT PASTA:** Attach fettuccine blades (to cut ¼-inch-wide strips) to pasta machine. Feed one end of driest pasta sheet (the first one you rolled out) into cutters, holding other end straight up, then catch strips from underneath machine before sheet goes completely through rollers and gently lay across floured baking sheets. (Alternatively, lightly flour strips and hang over backs of chairs.) Repeat with remaining sheets of pasta. Let pasta dry at least 5 minutes before cooking.

▶ **COOK PASTA:** Cook fettuccine in a 6- to 8-quart pot of well-salted boiling water until tender, about 2 minutes (do not over-cook). Drain.

**COOKS' NOTES:** The dough can be made (but not rolled out) 4 hours ahead and chilled, tightly wrapped in plastic wrap. Bring to room temperature before rolling out.

The fettuccine can be dried until leathery but still pliable, about 30 minutes, then chilled in sealable bags for up to 12 hours.

# Pizza Dough

*Adapted from Chris Bianco*

**Makes 1 (14-inch) pizza** | **Active time: 30 minutes** | **Start to finish: 1¾ hours**

This slightly wet dough, in conjunction with a hot pizza stone, produces a crisp yet chewy crust.

- 1¼ ounce package active dry yeast (2¼ teaspoons)
- 1¾ cups unbleached all-purpose flour, plus more for dusting
- ¾ cup warm water (105–115°F)
- 1 teaspoon salt
- ½ tablespoon extra-virgin olive oil

▶ Stir together yeast, 1 tablespoon flour, and ¼ cup warm water in a large bowl and let stand until surface appears creamy, about 5 minutes. (If mixture doesn't appear creamy, discard and start over with new yeast.)

▶ Add 1¼ cups flour, remaining ½ cup water, salt, and oil and stir until smooth. Stir in enough flour (¼ to ⅓ cup) for dough to begin to pull away from side of bowl. (Dough will be slightly wet.)

▶ Knead on a floured surface, lightly reflouring when dough becomes too sticky, until smooth, soft, and elastic, about 8 minutes. Form into a ball, put in a bowl, and dust with flour. Cover bowl with plastic wrap or a kitchen towel (not terry cloth) and let rise in a draft-free place at warm room temperature until doubled, about 1¼ hours.

**COOKS' NOTE:** The dough can be allowed to rise slowly in the refrigerator (instead of in a warm place) for 1 day. Bring to room temperature before shaping.

# Our Favorite Simple Polenta

Serves **8 to 10** | Active time: **15 minutes** | Start to finish: **1 hour**

Everyone loves this basic. For a richer version, add a little butter or grated Parmigiano-Reggiano before serving.

8  **cups water**

2  **teaspoons salt**

2  **cups polenta (not quick-cooking)**
   **or yellow cornmeal**

▶ Bring the water to a boil with the salt in a 4-quart heavy pot, then add the polenta in a thin stream, whisking. Cook over medium heat, whisking, 2 minutes. Reduce heat to low and simmer polenta, covered, stirring for 1 minute after every 10 minutes of cooking (a long-handled wooden spoon is helpful for this), 45 minutes total.

▶ Remove from heat and keep covered—polenta will stay warm and creamy for 20 minutes, but will begin to thicken and solidify if it stands longer.

# Basic Italian Vinaigrette

Makes ½ **cup** | Active time: **2 minutes** | Start to finish: **2 minutes**

Balance is the
key to a good
salad dressing.
Here's a classic.

2  **tablespoons red-wine vinegar**
½  **teaspoon salt**
⅛  **teaspoon black pepper**
5  **tablespoons extra-virgin olive oil**

▶ Whisk together vinegar, salt, and pepper in a bowl,
then add the oil in a slow stream, whisking until well
blended.

# CHAPTER 8

# MENUS

Every meal is a journey, but nowhere more so than in Italy, where dishes are presented in a carefully orchestrated sequence, and a meal unfolds like a compelling drama. On the pages that follow, you'll find menus inspired by particular regions and their specialties. Italian food is meant to be shared, so we've added step-by-step game plans and wine pairings that take the guesswork out of entertaining. When you prepare one of these menus, rich with the culinary traditions of its region, we hope you'll discover it creates an unmistakable sense of place—and the perfect dinner party.

# A ROMAN DINNER

Harbingers of spring, artichokes and lamb are also staples of the Roman table, famous for its robust flavors, ancient culinary traditions, and generous spirit. Garlic and thyme accent the first course of braised artichokes. Anchovy and rosemary infuse the second: tender lamb drizzled with piquant salsa verde and accompanied by pillowy semolina gnocchi, another Roman specialty. Each of these is served family-style, on a large platter to invite sharing and invoke the fellowship that's celebrated at every Italian meal. Crowning the feast is a layered macaroon cake that starts with beloved Italian ingredients—almonds, apricots, and mascarpone—but piles them high, American-style, into a spectacular multitiered confection.

## Menu
Serves 6

**Artichokes Braised with Garlic and Thyme**
(page 118)

**Anchovy and Rosemary Roasted Lamb with Salsa Verde**
(page 110)

**Souffléed Gnocchi**
(page 72)

**Roasted Fennel and Baby Carrots**
(page 122)

**Chiffonade of Romaine and Bibb Lettuces**
(page 114)

**Apricot Almond Macaroon Cake**
(page 158)

## Game Plan

**2 DAYS AHEAD**
▶ Make praline almonds
▶ Make apricot compote
▶ Make macaroon layers

**1 DAY AHEAD**
▶ Make salsa verde
▶ Make gnocchi but don't bake
▶ Wash and dry lettuces; chill in sealable plastic bags

**8½ HOURS AHEAD**
▶ Marinate lamb, chilled, 5 hours, then bring to room temperature
▶ Trim artichokes and chill in lemon water

**2 HOURS AHEAD**
▶ Roast lamb
▶ Trim fennel and carrots
▶ Make salad dressing

**30 MINUTES AHEAD**
▶ Cook artichokes

**WHILE LAMB RESTS**
▶ Increase oven to 450°F
▶ Roast fennel and carrots
▶ Bake souffléed gnocchi
▶ Assemble cake

**AFTER DINNER PLATES ARE CLEARED**
▶ Toss lettuces with dressing

## Wine Notes

For this menu, the whites will make a great beginning, the reds will best accompany the meat, and the sweet wine can be served either with the cake or on its own afterward.

**Splurge White: Fiorano Bianco or Semillon, Lazio ($100+)**
These phenomenal, wines—made from Malvasia and Semillon grapes—were barely available for many years but vintages from the 1980s on are now widely sold.

**Low-Commitment White: Villa Simone Frascati, Lazio ($12)**
This is the classic white of the Lazio region that surrounds Rome—light, thirst-quenching, and aromatic. Serve very cold.

**Splurge Red: Falesco *Montiano* Merlot, Lazio ($50)**
The signature flavors of this "Roman" Merlot are a perfect match for the roasted lamb.

**Low-Commitment Red: Terre Nere Etna Rosso, Sicily ($15)**
This Sicilian red, made from the Nerello Mascalese grape, has the cherry fruit flavors of a typical Pinot Noir, but is fuller bodied, earthy, dark, and spicy.

**Dessert Wine: Mastroberardino *Antheres,* Campania ($25)**
Spiked with black fruit, herbs, and bittersweet chocolate, this elixir is easy to sip on its own, but also adds another fruity element to the dessert on the plate.

# A VENETIAN DINNER

This culinary romp is inspired by the Veneto, a region that extends from the Venetian lagoon, with its abundance of sparkling seafood, all the way to the high Alps in the north. For a starter, woodsy mushrooms are served with white polenta, the latter a signature dish that came to the port of Venice in the sixteenth century. This is followed by succulent halibut, grilled simply with salt and pepper to allow its pure, clean flavor to shine through, and topped with tender beans and tomatoes from the garden. Throughout Italy, cheese and nuts often follow the salad; here, Pecorino and walnuts are tossed with shaved Brussels sprouts, combining two courses, American-style, into one. The feast comes to rest in the orchard, the source of the pear, quince, and apple that top a brown-sugar filling in a buttery crostata. (Recipes are adapted from Jonathan Waxman.)

## Menu

Serves 6

**Creamy White Polenta with Mushrooms and Mascarpone**
(page 74)

**Grilled Halibut with Fava Bean and Roasted Tomato Sauce**
(page 84)

**Shaved Brussels Sprout Salad**
(page 115)

**Pear, Apple, and Quince Crostata**
(page 155)

## Game Plan

**1 DAY AHEAD**

▶ Make bean and roasted tomato sauce for fish

▶ Toast walnuts for salad

▶ Roast fruit and make crostata dough

**6 HOURS AHEAD**

▶ Bake crostata

**3 HOURS AHEAD**

▶ Slice Brussels sprouts

**1 HOUR AHEAD**

▶ Season fish

▶ Bring bean and roasted tomato sauce to room temperature

▶ Make mushroom sauce for polenta

**JUST BEFORE SERVING**

▶ Cook polenta and reheat mushroom sauce

▶ Grill fish

▶ Toss together Brussels sprout salad

▶ Reheat crostata if desired

## Wine Notes

With this menu, choose either a white or a red and stick with it. There's no need to complicate the meal or fill your dishwasher with too many glasses. The sweet Recioto will make a nice sipper with the crostata or can be a dessert in itself.

**Splurge White: Inama Soave *Vigneto du Lot*, Veneto ($30)**
Many Soaves are flavorless and thin, but this single-vineyard "Super Soave" has a bouquet of orchard fruits, plus the texture and spices to pair nicely with the polenta and halibut.

**Low-Commitment White: Veronese *il Clandestino*, Veneto ($12)**
A casual, pleasant Garganega with crisp apple tones.

**Splurge Red: Quintarelli Valpolicella, Veneto ($75)**
Dark, decadent, juicy, ripe, spicy, complex: This Valpolicella from master winemaker Giuseppe Quintarelli is one of the Veneto's iconic wines.

**Low-Commitment Red: Allegrini *Palazzo della Torre*, Veneto ($16)**
Made from the same Corvina and Rondinella grapes used in Valpolicella, the Palazzo della Torre is a heady, deep red with luscious aromas.

**Dessert Wine: Tommasi Recioto della Valpolicella ($30)**
The sweet Recioto style dates back to the ancient Romans. It is a full, inky, portlike wine best served with a hint of chill.

# A TUSCAN DINNER

Bread and olive oil are hallmarks of Tuscan cooking, which is known for its rustic simplicity and pure, lusty flavors. Combined with roasted plum tomatoes to form *bruschette,* these down-to-earth ingredients provide a fitting start to a satisfying feast. Roast chicken with pancetta and black olives follows, accompanied by creamy polenta and broccoli rabe with sweet sausage. A salad of bitter greens refreshes the palate in anticipation of dessert—a custardy bread pudding made with pannetone and studded with brandy-soaked raisins. Taken as a whole, the meal is an artful illustration of the Italian principle of balance: The flavors complement but never repeat one another, and each contributes an essential note to the overall composition. (Recipes are adapted from Tony Oltranti.)

## Menu

Serves 8

Orange Negronis
(page 14)

Slow-Roasted-Tomato
Bruschette
(page 22)

Roast Chicken with
Pancetta and Olives
(page 94)

Broccoli Rabe with
Sweet Italian Sausage
(page 126)

Fennel, Frisée, and
Escarole Salad
(page 121)

Panettone Bread
Pudding
(page 146)

## Game Plan

**UP TO 2 WEEKS AHEAD**
▶Slow-roast tomatoes

**2 DAYS AHEAD**
▶Bake bread pudding

**1 DAY AHEAD**
▶Boil broccoli rabe
▶Wash and dry greens for salad and keep chilled in sealable plastic bags

**2 HOURS AHEAD**
▶Cut and toast or grill baguette slices
▶Start chicken

**1 HOUR AHEAD**
▶Make polenta
▶Make negronis when guests arrive

**20 MINUTES AHEAD**
▶Finish broccoli rabe
▶Make salad dressing

**JUST BEFORE SERVING**
▶Reheat bread pudding
▶Assemble *bruschette*

**AFTER DINNER PLATES ARE CLEARED**
▶Toss and serve salad

## Wine Notes

Open both the white and the red as your guests arrive, and let them choose. Both will benefit from aeration (pour them into decanters—they will only get better) and will accompany the meal nicely from start to finish. Save the sweet wines for dessert.

**Splurge White: Querciabella *Batàr*, Tuscany ($50)**
In this luxurious white, the Pinot Blanc grape delivers pear and citrus notes; the Chardonnay adds a full-bodied, creamy character with toasty, spicy flavors.

**Low-Commitment White: Fattoria le Pupille *Poggio Argentato*, Tuscany ($15)**
A blend of Traminer and Sauvignon Blanc, this zippy, bright, mineral-laden white hails from the Tuscan region of the Maremma.

**Splurge Red: Talenti Brunello di Montalcino Riserva ($60)**
The wine geeks at your table will know that you went big with this classic Tuscan Sangiovese.

**Low-Commitment Red: Talenti Rosso di Montalcino ($14)**
Many top-flight Brunello producers also make a budget-friendly wine from their younger vines. When it's not a grand dinner, this less complex Sangiovese will stand in nicely.

**Dessert Wine: Isole e Olena Vin Santo ($40)**
This wine—redolent of honey, caramel, raisins, and flowers, is a sweet splurge: Only a few barrels are made each vintage.

# The Italian Pantry

These basics are the building blocks of many recipes in this issue: Stock up!

▶ **ANCHOVIES:** The magic ingredient that helps create the underlying depth in so many Italian dishes. When sautéed in oil or butter, they dissolve into the fat. The most readily available fillets are packed in oil (in cans or jars) but whole anchovies packed in salt—which then have to be filleted—are also prized by the Italians and increasingly available by mail order. Anchovy paste is a substitute in a pinch, but be aware that it also contains vinegar, spices, and a bit of sugar.

▶ **ARBORIO RICE:** A medium-grain Italian rice, like Carnaroli and Vialone Nano, that is used to make risotto. As you stir the cooking rice, it releases its starch into the surrounding liquid, turning the mixture creamy while the kernel retains its shape and chewy texture.

▶ **BALSAMIC VINEGAR:** Along with red- and white-wine vinegars, a pantry essential. The finest *aceto balsamico tradizionale* comes from Modena and is used sparingly as a condiment. Less costly versions of varying quality are widely available and are fine for salads, marinades, and everyday use.

▶ **CANNED TOMATOES:** We rely on these workhorses of the Italian kitchen for most of the year because they are such a consistent and inexpensive product. We prefer whole tomatoes packed in juice, not in puree; a sauce made from the latter will be much heavier in texture and flavor. Many people like San Marzano tomatoes, but we've had good results with domestic brands. Be sure to check the label for sodium content, which can vary widely enough that you may need to lower the salt in a recipe.

▶ **CANNED TUNA:** Italian varieties packed in olive oil (some come in glass jars) are widely considered the most flavorful. It's a useful staple to have on hand for sauces and pastas, or to mix with white beans for a delicious salad or *bruschette* topping.

▶ **CAPERS:** The pickled flower buds of a Mediterranean shrub, prized for adding a salty, tangy flavor to sauces, salads, and pastas. Capers are either pickled in a vinegar brine or packed in coarse salt. Capers in brine need only be drained but those packed in salt should be rinsed well, then soaked for ½ hour; if they are still too salty, soak again in fresh water.

▶ **EXTRA-VIRGIN OLIVE OIL:** The term "extra-virgin" indicates oil that is freshly squeezed by a process known as "first press" or "cold press" (without heat or chemicals) and contains less than 1 percent acidity. Less expensive plain or "pure" olive oil is further refined with steam and chemicals. We prefer to use a supermarket extra-virgin such as Colavita or Bertolli for everyday cooking (not deep-frying) and save the more flavorful, often artisanal (and usually more expensive) versions like Seggiano for use in salad dressings and last-minute drizzles on seafood, vegetables, and *bruschette.*

▶ **NO-BOIL LASAGNE NOODLES:** One of the great culinary developments of the late twentieth century. Those made with egg, like Barilla, are amazingly close to the texture of homemade pasta. The manufacturers' instructions generally have you layer no-boil noodles in their dry state with a filling (usually a wetter one), but we've found that softening the noodles first in warm water works well for drier fillings and as a substitute for fresh pasta in cannelloni.

▶ **OLIVES:** Whether green or black, brine-cured or oil-cured, olives can stand alone as an antipasto or be added to dishes for their flavor and meaty texture. Commonly found Italian olives are black Gaetas—sold either oil-

cured (wrinkled) or brine-cured (smooth)—and green Cerignolas, also brine-cured (but any similarly cured Mediterranean olives will be good substitutes).

▶ **PANCETTA:** Italian-style pork belly or fresh bacon that's been salt-cured but not smoked. Most often it's rolled up pinwheel-style so that when sliced it has a spiral design. *Guanciale* ("gwan-*cha*-leh") is similar to pancetta but is made from the cheek, or jowl, of the pig. Both are used to flavor soups, sauces, stews, and many other dishes.

▶ **PASTA, FRESH AND DRIED:** Fresh and dried pasta are two very different products, and one isn't better than the other. Most fresh pasta is made with flour and eggs, and even when cooked al dente, it has a tender texture. Because of the eggs, the pasta swells substantially when cooked, so ½ pound will feed 4 people. Our favorite dried egg pasta is

Cipriani (available on Amazon.com and at specialty markets), but we also like De Cecco's egg fettuccine, which comes in nests. Creamy, buttery sauces are often tossed with egg pasta. Dried pasta generally refers to that made with hard durum wheat (semolina) flour and water (no egg) and extruded through factory machines into spaghetti, linguine, penne, etc. Durum wheat is what gives dried pasta its toothsome bite—it shouldn't be cooked to tender. It's often paired with tomato or oil-based sauces. In Italy, pasta of any type is not heavily sauced; the Italians appreciate the wheaty flavor of the noodles, and the sauce is meant to enhance it, not mask it.

▶ **PINE NUTS:** We favor Italian pignoli over other varieties for their smoother, less resinous flavor. Pine nuts can go rancid easily, so shop for them in a market where there's frequent turnover.

# Italian Cheeses

Nearly every region of Italy produces a distinctive cheese that pairs perfectly with the local dishes. Some are used for grating and cooking; others can be served as part of an antipasti platter or in a cheese course with bread, honey, nuts, and fresh or dried fruit.

▶ **FONTINA (ITALIAN):** A semi-firm cow's-milk cheese from Piedmont with a pronounced, deliciously nutty taste. Don't confuse it with Danish Fontina, which melts well but doesn't come near it in flavor.

▶ **GRANA PADANO:** A cow's-milk cheese similar to Parmigiano-Reggiano. It's not aged as long and is thus less distinctive in flavor, but it's much less expensive.

▶ **GORGONZOLA:** A soft cow's-milk blue from Lombardy, sold in two styles. Gorgonzola *dolce,* aged for 3 months, is softer and milder than the longer-aged Gorgonzola *naturale,* which is firmer and more pungent.

▶ **MASCARPONE:** Fresh, cultured cream that is used in both sweet and savory dishes. Its closest cousin is crème fraîche. The texture can vary, so if it's too thick, stir in some whipped cream to lighten it.

▶ **MOZZARELLA:** Known as "the flower of the milk," fresh mozzarella can be made from the milk of water buffalo (*mozzarella di bufala*) or cow. It's milky-sweet, moist, tender, very pliant, and incredibly tasty when eaten within a few hours of being made. Packaged supermarket mozzarella is rubbery and firm with no distinctive flavor, but it does melt well.

▶ **PARMIGIANO-REGGIANO:** The king of Italian cheeses. An aged, part-skim cow's-milk cheese artisanally made only in Emilia-Romagna and a small area of Lombardy. Most often grated over pasta, salads, and soups, it is also delicious in chunks as an antipasto. When shopping, look for "Parmigiano-Reggiano" stamped on the rind.

▶ **PECORINO ROMANO:** An aged sheep's-milk cheese made in the province surrounding Rome, though less expensive ones are made in Sardinia. (Locatelli, Fulvi, Brunelli, and Lopez are true Pecorino Romanos.) Though used like Parmigiano-Reggiano, it is sharper tasting and can be quite salty.

▶ **PROVOLONE:** American provolone is a mildly flavored, pale yellow sliced cheese. It's a far cry from true Italian provolone, which is sold young or aged in various shapes and has a sharp, slightly smoky flavor.

▶ **RICOTTA:** A fresh cheese, made from the whey of sheep's or water buffalo milk in Italy, and from cow's milk in the U.S. Fresh ricotta, available at Italian and upscale markets, is denser, richer, and drier than the tubs of ricotta sold in supermarkets.

▶ **TALEGGIO:** An extremely fragrant—okay, stinky—soft cow's-milk cheese with a mild, nutty taste. It melts beautifully.

# Deciphering Italian Wines

Flustered by wine lists? Stumped at the store? Consult our handy guide.

### If you like Champagne . . .

There are so many choices when it comes to Italian sparkling and *méthode champenoise* wines:

- ► Franciacorta from Lombardy
- ► Prosecco from the Veneto
- ► Sweet Moscato d'Asti and Brachetto from Piedmont
- ► Sweet and dry, white and red Lambrusco from Emilia-Romagna

### If you like Sauvignon Blanc (such as Loire Valley Sancerre) . . .

You prefer white wines with bright, lip-smacking acidity and cool climate flavors. Italy does this style in several regions:

- ► Cool styles of Friulano (formerly known as Tocai Friulano) from Friuli
- ► Bianchetta Genovese from Liguria
- ► Greco di Tufo from Campania
- ► Verdicchio from the Marche

### If you like Pinot Noir . . .

You prefer high-toned, red-fruited, understated red wines. There are several options from the North and the southern extremes of Italy:

- ► The classic style of Barbera and Dolcetto from Piedmont
- ► Nerello Mascalese from Sicily
- ► Cannonau (known as Grenache in other parts of the world) from Sardinia

### If you like young Cabernet Sauvignon . . .

You drink your Cab for the big, masculine structure, firm tannins, and dark berry fruit. These are some of Italy's big guns:

- ► Super Tuscans (anything that ends in *aia*: Sassicaia, Solaia, Brancaia, Lupicaia, and many more)
- ► Young Aglianico from Basilicata
- ► Sagrantino from Umbria

### If you like Red Zinfandel . . .

You prefer the rich, dark, juicy, jammy reds. Italy does this style with several different grape varietals:

- ► Amarone and Valpolicella Ripasso from the Veneto
- ► Primitivo from Puglia (purportedly the ancestor of Zinfandel)
- ► Negroamaro from Puglia

# Credits

**RECIPES AND TEXT**

Andrea Albin, Celia Barbour, Belinda Chang, Lillian Chou, Kay Chun, Ruth Cousineau, Gina Marie Miraglia Erlquez, Paul Grimes, Ian Knauer, Jane Daniels Lear, Amy Mastrangelo, Kemp Minifie, Lori Powell, Melissa Roberts, Maggie Ruggiero, Zanne Stewart, Alexis M. Touchet, John Willoughby, Shelton Wiseman

Recipes pages 20, 108, 148 are reprinted from the book *Italian Easy: Recipes from The River Café London* by Rose Gray and Ruth Rogers. Copyright © 2004 by Rose Gray and Ruth Rogers. Published by Clarkson Potter, a division of Random House, Inc.

**WINES NOTES**

Pages 177, 179, 181: Belinda Chang, General Manager and Wine Director of New York's The Monkey Bar

**BOOK DESIGN**

Margaret Swart

**PHOTOGRAPHY**

**Cover**: Jeffrey Schad and Chris Gentile. Food styling by Mariana Velasquez. Prop styling by Pamela Duncan Silver.

Quentin Bacon: pages 73, 111, 114, 119, 123, 158, 176

Roland Bello: pages 12, 19, 25, 29, 125, 129

Ditte Isager: page 39

John Kernick: pages 2, 15, 24, 37, 61, 75, 85, 89, 93, 120, 135, 155, 157, 178

David Loftus: pages 21, 109, 149

Marcus Nilsson: pages 14, 95, 121, 127, 143, 180

Jeffrey Schad and Chris Gentile: pages 32, 47–48, 52, 57, 78, 103, 112, 131, 137–138, 151, 162

Jonny Valiant: page 65

Mikkel Vang: pages 43, 141, 147

George Whiteside: page 174

Romulo Yanes: pages 17, 23, 26, 31, 35, 41, 45, 51, 55, 59, 67, 71, 77, 81, 83, 87, 91, 97, 99, 101, 105, 107, 117, 130, 133, 145, 153, 161

**GOURMET SPECIAL EDITIONS**

**Executive Director, Content Development** Catherine Kelley
**Design Directors** Wyatt Mitchell and Alyson Keeling Cameron
**Food Editor** Kemp Minifie
**Editorial Systems Director** Kristen Rayner
**Director of Studios** Jeffrey Schad
**Studio Coordinator** Jesse Newhouse

**CONDÉ NAST PUBLICATIONS**

**Editorial Director** Thomas J. Wallace
**Senior Vice President, Editorial Operations** Rick Levine
**Vice-President, Digital Magazine Development** Scott Dadich

**SPECIAL THANKS**

Christine Arzeno
Belinda Chang
Christopher Donnellan
Michelle Egan
Rose Gold
Christopher Jagger
James Mate
Julie Michalowski
Clare O'Shea
Pamela Duncan Silver
Mariana Velasquez
Alden Wallace

# INDEX